How to Start & Manage a Bed & Breakfast Business

A Practical Way to Start Your Own Business

by Jerre G. Lewis and Leslie D. Renn

How to Start & Manage
A Bed and Breakfast Business

Lewis & Renn Associates, Inc.

Business & Professional Publishing

10315 Harmony Drive
Interlochen, Michigan 49643
(231) 275-7287

Leslie D. Renn
President

Jerre G. Lewis
Secretary-Treasurer

ISBN # 978-1-57916-169-9
Library of Congress Catalog Card Number
99-094207

TABLE OF CONTENTS

Chapter 1

Introduction

Selecting the right Bed & Breakfast business opportunity requires careful, thorough evaluations of yourself. Owning your own business is as much a part of the American dream as owning a home, and for you, this urge represents one of life's most exciting challenges. This book is for those men and women who someday may go into business for themselves and for those who are already in business for themselves but wish to strengthen their entrepreneurial and managerial skills.

Entrepreneurs come in all shapes and sizes, personalities, and lifestyles. They are usually highly motivated, hard-working individuals who receive satisfaction from taking risks. Your business should interest you, not just be an income generator. Analyze your personal style. Do you like working with people? Are you a self starter, goal oriented, persistent, a risk taker, willing to work hard and long hours?

If you have been honest in evaluating yourself, you will now select the right type of business. Before you can determine which of the multitude of businesses is right for you to start, you must evaluate the businesses you want to start by asking these questions. Is the business area growing? How does the economy affect it? Who dominates its market? Once you have considered a business that satisfies your needs and interest you must prepare a formal business plan by following the outline given in this book.

Small businesses constitute a dynamic and critical sector of the U.S. economy. Every year in the United States more than 600,000 new businesses are launched by independent men and women eager to make their own decisions, express their own ideas, and be their own bosses. But running your own business is not as easy as it may seem. There can be problems with the inventory, or getting the right goods delivered on time. Yet, managing one's own business can be a personally and financially rewarding experience for an individual strong enough to meet the test. A person with stamina, maturity, and creativity, one who is willing to make sacrifices, may find making a go of a struggling enterprise an exhilarating challenge with many compensations.

Small business owners are a dedicated group of people who work hard and whose hours on the job usually exceed the nine-to-five routine. The owner's commitment is the key to many successful small businesses; an entrepreneur is able to communicate ideas, lead, plan, be patient, and work well with people.

Managing a business requires more than the possession of technical knowledge. Because most small businesses are started by technical people, such as engineers and salesmen, their managerial acumen is often less developed than their technical skills. The need to plan for management is common to every type of and size of business, and there are certain steps that must be taken. Although some of them are very elementary — such as applying for a city business permit — the most important are often complex and difficult and require the advice of specialists: accountants, attorneys, insurance brokers, and/or bankers. For almost any business though, the first step will be to translate the entrepreneur's basic idea into a concrete plan for action.

To gauge your level of entrepreneurial spirit, the following quiz was created. Please answer each question honestly and then total the columns.

ENTREPRENEURIAL QUIZ

	YES	NO	SOMETIMES
1. I am a self-starter. Nobody has to tell me how to get going.	____	____	_____
2. I am capable of getting along with just about everybody.	____	____	_____
3. I have no trouble getting people to follow my lead.	____	____	_____
4. I like to be in charge of things and see them through.	____	____	_____
5. I always plan ahead before beginning a project. I am usually the one who gets everyone organized.	____	____	_____
6. I have a lot of stamina. I can keep going as long as necessary.	____	____	_____
7. I have no trouble making decisions and can make up my mind in a hurry.	____	____	_____
8. I say exactly what I mean. People can trust me.	____	____	_____
9. Once I make my mind up to do something, nothing can stop me.	____	____	_____
10. I am in excellent health and have a lot of energy.	____	____	_____

	YES	NO	SOMETIMES

11. I have experience or technical knowledge in the business I intend to start.

12. I feel comfortable taking risks if it is something I really believe in.

13. I have good communication skills.

14. I am flexible in my dealings with people and situations.

15. I consider myself creative and resourceful.

16. I can analyze a situation and take steps to correct problems.

17. I think I am capable of maintaining a good working relationship with employees.

18. I am not a dictator. I am willing to listen to employees, customers and suppliers.

19. I am not rigid in my policies. I am willing to adjust to meet the needs of employees, customers, and suppliers.

20. More than anything else, I want to run my own business.

Total of Column #1   _____

Total of Column #2   _____

Total of Column #3   _____

If the total of Column #1 is the highest, then you will probably be very successful in running your own business.

If the total of Column #2 is the highest, you may find that running a business is more than you can handle.

If the total of Column #3 is the highest, you should consider taking on a partner who is strong in your weak areas.

NOTE: This quiz was adapted from the Small Business Administration publication *Checklist for Going Into Business.*

Notes _____

Chapter 2

Planning the Business

The Dream of self-employment can be fulfilled. You don't need to finance the opening of an elaborate office or facility to start your own one-person corporation either. You can start your own Bed & Breakfast business.

Anyone preparing to run an Bed & Breakfast business needs to learn a great deal to assure the best possible chance for success.

GETTING STARTED

The following is a list of what you need to accomplish to insure that your Bed & Breakfast endeavor will head in the right direction.

1. Define your educational background and work experience.

2. Survey all the basic types of Bed & Breakfast businesses.

3. Define what products or services your Bed & Breakfast business will be marketing.

4. Define who will be using your products/services.

5. Define why they will be purchasing your products/services.

6. List all competitors in your Bed & Breakfast marketing area.

ZONING REGISTRATIONS

Bed & Breakfast businesses are subject to many laws and regulations enforced by state, county, township governmental units. Most jurisdictions now have codes, a zoning board, and an appeal board which regulate businesses. Areas often are zoned residential, commercial or industrial.

You must become familiar with these regulations. If you are doing business in violation of these regulations, you could be issued a cease and desist order or fined.

Certain kinds of goods cannot be produced in the home, though these restrictions vary somewhat from state-to-state. Most states outlaw home production of fireworks, drugs, poisons, explosives, sanitary/medical products and some toys.

Many localities have registration requirements for new businesses. You will need to obtain a work certificate or license from the state.

TAX REQUIREMENTS

Application for Employer Identification Number, Form SS-4. This registers you with the Internal Revenue Service as a business. If you have employees, you should ask for Circular E along with your ID number. Circular E explains federal income and social security tax withholding requirements.

Employer's Annual Unemployment Tax Return, Form 940. This is only if you have employees. It's used to report and pay the Federal Unemployment Compensation Tax.

Employee's Withholding Allowance Certificate, W-4. Every employee must complete the W-4 so the proper amount of income tax can be withheld from the employee's pay. If the employee claims more than 15 allowances or a complete withholding exemption while having a salary of more than $200 a week, a copy of the W-4 must go to the IRS.

Employer's Wage and Tax Statement, W-2. Used to report to the IRS the total taxes withheld and total compensation paid to each employee per year.

Reconciliation/Transmittal of Income and Tax Statements, W-3. Used to total all information from the W-2. Sent to the Social Security Administration.

The IRS puts on monthly workshops on understanding and using these forms. Call your local IRS office for further information.

States also have various tax form requirements including: an unemployment tax form, a certificate of registration application, a sales and use tax return, an employer's quarterly contribution and payroll report, an income tax withholding registration form, an income tax withholding form, and others. Some forms apply only to employers who have employees. Your local IRS office and state Office of Taxation can provide you with listings of forms you will need to start your business. The following table outlines Federal tax form requirements.

Every small business begins with an idea — a product to be manufactured or sold, a service to be performed.

Whatever the business or its degree of complexity, the owner needs a business plan in order to transform a vision into a working operation.

This business plan should describe in writing and in figures the proposed Bed & Breakfast business and its products, services, or manufacturing processes. It should also include an analysis of the market, a marketing strategy, an organizational plan, and measurable financial objectives.

WHAT SHOULD A BUSINESS PLAN COVER?

It should be a thorough and objective analysis of both personal abilities and business requirements for a particular product or service. It should define strategies for such functions as marketing and production, organization and legal aspects, accounting and finance. A business plan should answer such questions as:

What do I want and what am I capable of doing?
What are the most workable ways of achieving my goals?
What can I expect in the future?

There is no single best way to begin. What follows is simply a guide and can be changed to suit individual needs.

1. Define Long-term goals.
2. State short-term.
3. Set marketing strategies to meet goals and objectives.
4. Analyze available resources.
5. Assemble financial data.
6. Review plan.

Please refer to Figure 2.1 for a complete business plan outline.

The business operator with a realistic plan has the best chance for success.

Figure 2.1

BUSINESS PLAN FOR SMALL BUSINESSES

    I.   Type of Business

    II.   Location

    III.   Target Market

    IV.   Planning Process

    V.   Organizational Structure

    VI.   Staffing Procedures

    VII.   Market Strategy

    IX.   Financial Planning

    X.   Budgeted Balance Sheet

    XI.   Budgeted Income Statement

    XII.   Budgeted Cash Flow Statement

    XIII.   Break-Even Chart

Notes

Chapter 3

Marketing Strategies
for an Bed & Breakfast Business

As a potential Bed & Breakfast business owner, it is important to learn all you can about marketing. You will need to know how to identify your market and how to market your product or service.

As a business person who looks for a profit from the sale of goods, you recognize that without people who want to buy, there is no demand for the things you want to sell. Thus, it is important that, in addition to knowing about the functions of marketing, you also study the activities that will influence the consumer. When you satisfy the specific needs and wants of the customer, then he or she may be willing to pay you a price that will include a profit for you — and to make a profit is one of the reasons you have become an Bed & Breakfast business owner. Although there are many activities connected with marketing, most of them can be classified in these categories: buy, finance, transport, standardize, store, insure, advertise and sell.

Target Market Analysis

Before you can create a successful marketing campaign, it's necessary to determine your target market (toward whom to direct your energies). The whole concept of target marketing can seem very scary at first. On the surface, targeting appears to be limiting the scope of the pool of potential customers. Many people fear that by defining a market, they will lose business. They are concerned that they will choose the wrong market. Or that other practitioners will take just anybody and therefore some of their business.

You must keep in mind that the purpose of defining your target market is to make your life easier and increase the productivity of your promotional endeavors. Many opportunities exist in this world and it's impossible to pursue them all or be everything to everyone. You need to know where to focus your energy and money when it comes to promotion and advertising.

The two most common means of market analysis are demographics and psychographics, which describe a person in terms of objective data and personality attributes.

Demographics are statistics such as:
- age
- gender
- income level
- geographic location
- occupation
- education level

Psychographics are lifestyle factors including:
- special interest activities
- philosophical beliefs
- social factors
- cultural involvements

The more you know about your potential customers, the easier it is to develop an appropriate position statement and design an effective marketing campaign. The actual number of target markets you have depends mainly upon the size of your practice and the scope of your knowledge.

Your Target Market Profile

In order to clarify your target market(s) you need to delineate the demographic and psychographic factors and then identify the characteristics your customers have in common.

Describe your current customers and those who are most likely your future customers:

What is the age range and average age of your customers?

What is the percentage of males?

What is the percentage of females?

What is the average educational level of your customers?

Where do your customers live?

What are the occupations of your customers?

Where do your customers work?

What is the average annual income level of your customers?

Of what special interest groups are your customers members?

What is the primary reason your customers use your services?

Defining Your Target Market(s)

Write a descriptive statement for each of your target markets (refer to your "Target Market Profile"). Include a brief overview of the services you are providing to that group and a detailed analysis of the characteristics of the specific clientele.

Target Market 1:

Target Market 2:

Target Market 3:

Bed & Breakfast Business Marketing

The foundation for creating a thriving customer base.

A. Overview

This section is about clarifying your beliefs and attitudes toward your profession and determining the image you wish to portray.

1. Describe the "character" that you want for your business.
   Depict the image you want to convey:

2. State your philosophy in regard to your business:

3. Describe your philosophy regarding your practice in business:

B. Customer Profile

This is a descriptive analysis of your current and potential customers — who they are, what their interests are, and where you can find them. Include each of your target markets.

1. Target Market 1:

2. Target Market 2:

3. Target Market 3:

C. Competition's Marketing Assessment

The first phase in planning your promotional campaign is appraising the competition. List each of your major competitors and describe the marketing strategies they utilize. Be certain to include where and how often they advertise.

1. Major Competitor 1:

2. Major Competitor 2:

3. Major Competitor 3:

4. Major Competitor 4:

5. Major Competitor 5:

6. Major Competitor 6:

Bed & Breakfast Marketing Planning

Outline for Marketing:

I.   Produce/Service Concept
    A. Name of produce or service
    B. Descriptive characteristics of product or service
    C. Unit sales
    D. Analysis of market trends

II. Number of Customers in Market Area:
    A. Profile of customers
    B. Average customer expenditure
    C. Total market

III. Your Market Potential:
    A. Total market divided by competition
    B. Total market multiplied by percent who will buy your product

IV. Needs of Customers:
    A. Identification
    B. Pleasure
    C. Social approval
    D. Personal interest
    E. Price

V.   Direct Marketing Sources:
    A. Trade magazines
    B. Trade associates
    C. Small Business Administration (SBA)
    D. Government publications
    E. Yellow Pages
    F. Marketing directories

VI. Customer Profile:
    A. Geographical
    B. Gender
    C. Age range
    D. Income brackets
    E. Occupation
    F. Educational level

Chapter 4

Promoting the Bed & Breakfast Business

When a new business is opened, the owner must be prepared to publicize the business or its chance for success will be slim. Only a few businesses — such as those with a prime location, nationally known name, or a built-in clientele — can succeed without advertising to promote market awareness and stimulate sales.

The first purpose — promoting customer awareness — applies as much to established businesses as to newcomers.

In the Bed & Breakfast business, you will find it easier to retain old customers than to win new ones. When old customers move away from your area, or when their buying needs change, you need new customers to maintain your sales volume. If you expect your business to gain, you will need additional new customers. New customers are those who move into your area or who have grown into your line of products because now they can afford them or they need them. We see advertising and we hear advertising all around us, and yet that is only a part of it. Through advertising, you call the attention of customers to your products.

As a small business owner, you may advertise your business through your location. People pass by and are attracted to your operation because of what you are selling. To get a better idea of what advertising is, consider some of the following functions of advertising:

1. *To inform:* Letting customers know what you have for sale through brochures, leaflets, newspapers, radio, TV, and etc.

2. *Persuade:* Persuasion is the art of leading individuals to do what you want them to do. There are sales personnel who have persuasive sales presentations, but persuasion in advertising is nonpersonal. The appeal is made through the printed or spoken words or a picture. The influence of an ad on readers occurs as purchasers choose what they want among different products, and different wants. To gain the actions you want — <u>a sale</u> — you must persuade a customer to examine personally what you have for sale.

3. *Reminder:* Advertising performs it's third function when it reminds those who have been persuaded to buy once that the same product will bring satisfaction. The ad will also remind a customer of the characteristics of a product purchased some time ago, and where he or she bought it. Because customers change their loyalty to a place of business, their taste for products, and often their trading area patronage, advertising is necessary to draw new customers and to hold old customers. To generate results from advertising that will be profitable to your business, you will have to produce answers to the what, where and how of advertising.

What to Advertise

The nature of your business will partially answer the question "Shall I advertise goods or services?" What are the outstanding features of your business? Is it unique in any way? Does it have strong points? Do you have something to offer that the competition is not able to duplicate? Answers to these questions will give you a start in deciding what to advertise.

Where to Advertise

Of course, you will want to advertise within your marketing area, however there are a few guidelines to remember:

A. Who are your customers?

B. What is their income range?

C. Why do they buy?

D. How do they buy? Do they pay Cash? Charge?

E. What is the radius of your market area?

How to Advertise:

In determining how to advertise, you will have to consider your dollar allocation for advertising and the media suitable to your particular kind of business. However, it is important to have a balance between the presentation of the product or service being advertised and the application of three basic principles.

1. Gain the attention of the audience.

2. Establish a need.

3. Tell where that need may be filled.

See Figure A for an outline of the different advertising media and Figure B for budget on media goals.

Advertising Media

Media	Market Coverage	Type of Audience
Daily Newspaper	Single community or entire metro area; zoned editions sometimes available	General
Weekly Newspaper	Single community	Residents
Telephone Directory	Geographical area or occupational field served by the directory	Active shoppers for goods or services
Direct mail audience	Controlled by the advertiser	Controlled
Radio audience	Definable market area	Selected
Television audience	Definable market area	Various
Outdoor	Entire metro area	General auto drivers
Magazine	Entire metro area or magazine region	Selected audience

Figure A

Promotion and Advertising Plan — Bed & Breakfast Business

In designing your promotional plan, it's wise to use a variety of media. You must have specific goals, time lines and budgets for each marketing application

Media	Goal	Timeline	Budget

Notes

Chapter 5

Financial Planning for an Bed & Breakfast Business

Financial planning is the process of analyzing and monitoring the financial performance of your business so you can assess your current position and anticipate future problem areas. The daily, monthly, seasonal, and yearly operation of your business requires attention to the figures that tell you about the firm's financial health.

Maintaining good financial records is a necessary part of doing business.

The increasing number of governmental regulations alone makes it virtually impossible to avoid keeping detailed records. Just as important is to keep them for yourself. The success of your business depends on them. An efficient system of record keeping can help you to:

- make management decisions
- compete in the marketplace
- monitor performance
- keep track of expenses
- eliminate unprofitable merchandise
- protect your assets
- prepare your financial statements

Financial skills should include understanding of the balance sheet, the profit-and-loss statement, cash flow projection, break-even analysis, and source and application of funds. In many businesses, the husband and wife run the business; it is especially important that both of them understand financial management. Most small business owners are not accountants, but they must understand the tool of financial management if they are going to be able to measure the return on their investment. Although good records are essential to good financial planning, they alone are not enough because their full use requires interpretation and analysis. The owner/manager's financial decisions concerning return on invested funds, approaches to banks, securing greater supplier credit, raising additional equity capital and so forth, can be more successful if he takes the time to develop understanding and use of the balance sheet and profit-and-loss statement.

Balance Sheet:

The balance sheet, Figure I, shows the financial condition of a business at the end of business on a specific day. It is called a balance sheet because the total assets balance with, or are equal to, total liabilities plus owner's capital balance. Current assets are those that the owner does not anticipate holding for long. This category includes cash, finished goods in inventory, and accounts receivable. Fixed assets are long-term assets, including plant and equipment. A third possible category is the intangible asset of goodwill. Liabilities are debts owed by the business, including both accounts payable, which are usually short-term, and notes payable, which are usually long-term debts such as mortgage payments. The difference between the value of the assets and the value of the liabilities is the capital. This category includes funds invested by the owner plus accumulated profits, less withdrawals.

The Income Statement:

This statement, Figure II, is also known as a profit-and loss (P&L) statement. It shows how a business has performed over a certain period of time. An income statement specifies sales, costs of sales, gross profit, expenses and net income or loss from operations.

Figure I

Financial Forecast

Opening Balance Sheet - Date

ASSETS

Current Assets

Cash and bank accounts		$
Accounts receivable		$
Inventory		$
Other current assets		$ _____
TOTAL CURRENT ASSETS	(A)	$ _____

Fixed Assets

Property owned		$
Furniture and equipment		$
Business automobile		$
Leasehold improvements		$
Other fixed assets		$ _____
TOTAL FIXED ASSETS	(B)	$ _____
TOTAL ASSETS	(A+B = X)	$ _____

LIABILITIES

Current Liabilities (due within the next 12 months)

Bank loans		$
Other loans		$
Accounts payable		$
Other current liabilities		$ _____
TOTAL CURRENT LIABILITIES	(C)	$ _____

Long-term Liabilities

Mortgages		$
Long-term loans		$
Other long-term liabilities		$ _____
TOTAL LONG-TERM LIABILITIES	(D)	$ _____
TOTAL LIABILITIES	(C+D = Y)	$ _____
NET WORTH	(X-Y = Z)	$ _____
TOTAL NET WORTH AND LIABILITIES	(Y+Z)	$ _____

Figure II

Business Income and Expense Forecast for the Next 12 Months

One year estimate ending _____ , 19 _____

Projected Number of Clients

For your services   _____

For your products   _____

TOTAL NUMBER OF CLIENTS   _____

Projected Income

Sessions $ _____

Product sales $ _____

Other $ _____

TOTAL INCOME $ _____

Projected Expenses

Start-up costs $ _____

Monthly expenses (x 12) $ _____

Annual expenses $ _____

TOTAL EXPENSES $ _____

TOTAL OPERATING PROFIT (OR LOSS) $ _____

CAPITAL REQUIRED FOR THE NEXT 12 MONTHS $ _____

Bed & Breakfast Business

Start-Up Costs Worksheet	
Item	**Estimated Expense**
Open checking account	$
Telephone installation	$
Equipment	$
First & last month's rent, security deposit, etc.	$
Supplies	$
Business cards, stationery, etc.	$
Advertising and promotion package	$
Decorating and remodeling	$
Furniture and fixtures	$
Legal and professional fees	$
Insurance	$
Utility deposits	$
Beginning inventory	$
Installation of fixtures and equipment	$
Licenses and permits	$
Other	$
TOTAL	$

Fixed Annual Expense Worksheet	
Item	**Estimated Expense**
Property insurance	$
Business auto insurance	$
Licenses and permits	$
Liability insurance	$
Disability insurance	$
Professional society membership	$
Fees (legal, accounting, etc.)	$
Taxes	$
Other	$
TOTAL	$

Monthly Business Expense Worksheet		
Expense	**Estimated Monthly Cost**	**X 12**
Rent	$	$
Utilities	$	$
Telephone	$	$
Bank fees	$	$
Supplies	$	$
Stationery and business cards	$	$
Networking club dues	$	$
Education (seminars, books professional journals, etc.)	$	$
Business car (Payments, gas, repairs, etc)	$	$
Advertising and promotion	$	$
Postage	$	$
Entertainment	$	$
Repair, cleaning and maintenance	$	$
Travel	$	$
Business loan payments	$	$
Salary/Draw	$	$
Staff salaries	$	$
Miscellaneous	$	$
Taxes	$	$
Professional fees	$	$
Decorations	$	$
Furniture and fixtures	$	$
Equipment	$	$
Inventory	$	$
Other	$	$
TOTAL MONTHLY	$	$
TOTAL YEARLY		$

Cash Flow Forecast						
	January Estimate	**January Actual**	**February Estimate**	**February Actual**	**March Estimate**	**March Actual**
Beginning cash						
Plus monthly income from: Fees						
Sales						
Loans						
Other						
TOTAL CASH AND INCOME						
Expenses:						
Rent						
Utilities						
Telephone						
Bank fees						
Supplies						
Stationery and business cards						
Insurance						
Dues						
Education						
Auto						
Advertising and promotion						
Postage						
Entertainment						

	January Estimate	January Actual	February Estimate	February Actual	March Extimate	March Actual
Repair and maintenance						
Travel						
Business loan payments						
Licenses and permits						
Salary/Draw						
Staff salaries						
Taxes						
Professional fees						
Decorations						
Furniture and fixtures						
Equipment						
Inventory						
Other Expenses						
TOTAL EXPENSES						
ENDING CASH (+/-)						

Cash Flow Forecast (Continued)

Notes

Chapter 6

Bed & Breakfast Business Planning

Introduction

Our increasingly service oriented economy offers a widening spectrum of opportunities for customized and personalized small business growth. Though untrained entrepreneurs have traditionally had a high rate of failure, small businesses can be profitable. Success in a small Bed & Breakfast business is not an accident. It requires both skills in a service or product area and acquisition of management and attitudinal competencies.

The purpose of this publication is to help you take stock of your interests, aptitudes and skills. Many people have good business ideas but not everyone has what it takes to succeed. If you are convinced that a profitable Bed & Breakfast business is attainable, this publication will provide step-by-step guidance in development of the basic written business plan.

Information Gathering

A helpful tool for use in determining if you are ready to take the risks of an Bed & Breakfast business operation is the SMA publication entitled *Going Into Business* (MP-12).

It will help you focus on the basic steps in information gathering and business planning.

Careful planning is required to research legal and tax issues, proper space utilization and to establish time management discipline. Inadequate or careless attention to development of a detailed business plan can be costly for you and your family in terms of lost time, wasted talent and disappearing dollars.

The Entrepreneurial Personality

A variety of experts have documented research that indicates that successful small business entrepreneurs have some common characteristics. How do you measure up? On this checklist, write a "Y" if you believe the statement describes you; a "N" if it doesn't; and a "U" if you can't decide:

_____ I have a strong desire to be my own boss.

_____ Win lose or draw, I want to be master of my own financial destiny.

_____ I have significant specialized business ability based on both my education and my experience.

_____ I have an ability to conceptualize the whole of a business; not just its individual parts, but how they relate to each other.

_____ I develop an inherent sense of what is "right" for a business and have the courage to pursue it.

_____ One or both of my parents were entrepreneurs; calculate risk-taking runs in the family.

_____ My life is characterized by a willingness and capacity to preserver.

_____ I possess a high level of energy, sustainable over long hours to make the business successful.

While not every successful Bed & Breakfast business owner starts with a "Y" answer to all of these questions, three or four "N"s and "U"s should be sufficient reason for you to stop and give a second thought to going it alone. Many proprietors who sense entrepreneurial deficiencies seek extra training a support their limitations with help from a skilled team of business advisors such as accountants, bankers and attorneys.

Selecting a Business

A logical first step for the undecided is to list potential areas of personal background, special training, education and job experience, and special interests that could be developed into a business. Review the following list of activities which have proven marketable for others. On a scale of "0" (no interest or strength) to "10" (maximum interest or strength) indicate the potential for you and a total score for each activity.

Time Management

For both the novice and the experienced business person planning a small Bed & Breakfast enterprise, an early concern requiring self-evaluation is time management.

It is very difficult for some people to make and keep work schedules even in a disciplined office setting. As your own boss the problem can be much greater. To determine how much time you can devote to your business, begin by drafting a weekly task timetable listing all current and potential responsibilities and the blocks of time required for each. When and how can business responsibilities be added without undue physical or mental stress on you or your family? Potential conflicts must be faced and resolved at the outset and as they occur, otherwise your business can become a nightmare. During the first year of operation, continue to chart, post and checkoff tasks on a daily, weekly and monthly basis.

Distractions and excuses for procrastination abound. It is important to keep both a planning and operating log. These tools will help avoid oversights and provide vital information when memory fails.

To improve the quality of work time, consider installation of a telephone line for the business and attaching an answering machine to take messages when you do not wish to be distracted or are away from your business. A business line has the added advantage of allowing you to have a business listing in the phone book and if you wish to buy it, an ad in the classified directory.

Is an Bed & Breakfast Business Site Allowable?

Now you will want to investigate potential legal and community problems associated with operating the business. You should gather, read and digest specialized information concerning federal, state, county and municipal laws and regulations concerning Bed & Breakfast business operations.

Check first! Get the facts in writing. Keep a topical file for future reference. Some facts and forms will be needed for your business plan. There may be limitations enforced that can make your planned business impossible or require expensive modifications to your property.

Items to be investigated, recorded and studied are:

TO DO   DONE

_____   _____   county or city zoning code restrictions

_____   _____   necessary permits and licenses for operation

_____   _____   state and local laws and codes regarding zoning

_____   _____   deed or lease restrictions such as covenants and restrictive conditions of purchase

_____	_____	parking and customer access; deliveries
_____	_____	sanitation, traffic and noise codes
_____	_____	signs and advertising
_____	_____	state and federal code requirements for space, ventilation, heat and light
_____	_____	limitations on the number and type of workers. If not, check with the local Chamber of Commerce office
_____	_____	reservations that neighbors may have about a business next to or near them

Here are some ways to collect your information. Call or visit the zoning office at county headquarters or city hall. In some localities the city or county Office of Economic Development has print materials available to pinpoint key "code" items affecting a business.

Even in rural areas, the era of unlimited free enterprise is over. Although the decision makers may be in the state capital or in a distant regional office of a federal agency, check before investing in inventory, equipment or marketing programs. If in doubt, call the state office of Industrial Development or the nearest SBA district office. In some states the county agent or home demonstration agent will have helpful information concerning rural or farm business development.

Is the Business Site Insurable?

In addition to community investigations, contact your insurance company or agent. It is almost certain that significant changes will be required in your coverage and limits when you start a business. When you have written a good description of your business, call your agent for help in insuring you properly against new hazards resulting from your business operations such as:

37

- Fire, theft and casualty damage to inventories and equipment
- business interruption coverage
- fidelity bonds for employees
- liability for customers, vendors and others visiting the business
- workmen's compensation
- group health and life insurance
- product liability coverage if you make or sell a product; workmanship liability for services
- business use of vehicle coverage

Overall Bed & Breakfast Site Evaluation

After you have gathered as much information as seems practical you may wish to evaluate several different locations. Here's a handy checklist. Using the "0" to "10" scale, grade these vital factors:

Factors to Consider

Factor   **Grades 0-10**

1. Customer convenience   _____

2. Availability of merchandise or raw materials   _____

3. Nearby competition   _____

4. Transportation availability and rates   _____

5. Quality and quantity of employees available   _____

6. Availability of parking facilities   _____

7. Adequacy of utilities (sewer, water, power, gas)   _____

8. Traffic flow   _____

9. Tax burden   _____

10. Quality of police and fire services   _____

11. Environmental factors   _____

12. Physical suitability for future expansion   _____

13. Provision for future expansion   _____

14. Vendor delivery access   _____

15. Personal convenience   _____

16. Cost of operation   _____

17. Other factors including how big you get without moving   _____

TOTALS   _____

Writing the Business Plan

Now that your research and plan development is nearing completion, it is time to move into action. If you are still in favor of going ahead, it is time to take several specific steps. The key one is to organize your dream scheme into a business plan.

What is it?

- As a business plan it is written by the Bed & Breakfast business owner with outside help as needed
- It is accurate and concise as a result of careful study
- It explains how the business will function in the marketplace
- It clearly depicts its operational characteristics
- It details how it will be financed
- It outlines how it will be managed
- It is the management and financial "blueprint" for start-up and profitable operation
- It serves as a prospectus for potential investors and lenders

Why create it?

- The process of putting the business plan together, including the thought that you put in before writing it, forces you to take an objective, critical, unemotional look at your entire business proposal
- The finished written plan is an operational tool which, when properly used, will help you manage your business and work toward its success
- The completed business plan is a means for communicating your ideas to others and provides the basis for financing your business

Who should write it?

- The Bed & Breakfast owner to the extend possible
- Seek assistance in weak areas, such as:
  - accounting
  - insurance
  - capital requirements
  - operational forecasting
  - tax and legal requirements

When should a business plan be used?

- To make crucial start-up decisions
- To reassure lenders or backers
- To measure operations progress
- To test planning assumptions
- As a basis for adjusting forecasts
- To anticipate ongoing capital and cash requirements
- As the benchmark for good operations management

Proposed Outline for Bed & Breakfast Business Plan

This outline is suggested for a small proprietorship or family business. Shape it to fit *your* unique needs. For more complex manufacturing or franchise operations see the Resource section for other options.

Part I - Business Organization

Cover page:

    A.   Business name:

            Street address:

            Mailing address:

            Telephone number:

            Owner(s) name(s):

Inside pages:

    B.   Business form:

            (proprietorship, partnership, corporation)

            If incorporated (state incorporation)

            Include copies of key subsidiary documents in an appendix.

Remember even partnerships require written agreements of terms and conditions to avoid later conflicts and to establish legal entities and equities. Corporations require charters, articles of incorporation and bylaws.

Part II - Business Purpose and Function

In this section, write an accurate yet, concise description of the business. Describe the business you plan to start in narrative form.

What is the principal activity? Be specific. Give product or service description(s):

- retail sales?

- manufacturing?

- service?

- other?

How will it be started?

- a new start up

- the expansion of an existing business

- purchase of a going business

- a franchise operation

- actual or projected start up date

Why will it succeed? Promote your idea!

- how and why this business will be successful

- what is unique about your business

- what is its market "niche"

What is your experience in this business? If you have a current resume of your career, include it in an appendix and reference it here. Otherwise write a narrative here and include a resume in the finished product. If you lack specific experience, detail how you plan to gain it, such as training, apprenticeship or working with partners who have experience.

The Marketing Plan

The marketing plan is the core of your business rationale. To develop a consistent sales growth an Bed & Breakfast business person much become knowledgeable about the market. To demonstrate your understanding, this section of the Bed & Breakfast business plan should seek to concisely answer several basic questions:

Who is your market?

- Describe the profile of your typical customer
  Age?
  Male, female, both?
  How many in family?
  Annual family income?
  Location?
  Buying patterns?
  Reason to buy from you?

Other?

- Biographically describe your trading area (i.e., county, state, national)

- Economically describe your trading area: (single family, average earnings, number of children)

How large is the market?

- Total units or dollars?

- Growing ____ Steadily ____ Decreasing ____

- If growing, annual growth rate. _____

Who is your competition?

No small business operates in a vacuum. Get to know and respect the competition. Target your marketing plans. Identify direct competitors (both in terms of geography and product lines), and those who are similar or marginally comparative. Begin by listing names, addresses and products or service. Detail briefly but concisely the following information concerning each of your competitors:

- Who are the nearest ones?

- How are their businesses similar or competitive to yours?

- Do you have a unique "niche"? Describe it.

- How will your service or product be better or more saleable than your competitors?

- Are their businesses growing? Stable? Declining? Why?

- What can be learned from observing their operations or talking to their present or former clients?

- Will you have competitive advantages or disadvantages? Be honest!

What percent of the market will you penetrate?

1. estimate the market in total units or dollars

2. estimate your planned volume

3. amount your volume will add to total market

4. subtract 3 from 2

Item 4 represents the amount of your planned volume that must be taken away from the competition.

What pricing and sales terms are you planning?

The primary consideration in pricing a product or service is the value that it represents to the customer. If, on the previous checklist of features, your product is truly ahead of the field, you can command a premium price. On the other hand, if it is a "me too" product, you may have to "buy" a share of the market to get your foothold and then try to move price up later. This is always risky and difficult. One rule will always hold: ultimately, the market will set the price. If your selling price does not exceed your costs and expenses by the margin necessary to keep your business healthy, you will fail. Know your competitors pricing policies. Send a friend to comparison shop. Is there discounting? Special sales? Price leaders? Make some "blind" phone calls. Detail your pricing policy.

What is your sales plan?

Describe how you will sell, distribute or service what you sell. Be specific. Below are outlined some common practices:

Direct Sales - by telephone or in person. The tremendous growth of individual sales representatives who sell by party bookings, door to door, and through distribution of call back promotional campaigns suggests that careful research is required to be profitable.

Mail Order - Specialized markets for leisure time or unique products have grown as more two income families find less time to shop. Be aware of recent mail order legislation and regulation.

Franchising -

a. You may decide to either buy into someone else's franchise as a franchisee, or

b. Create your own franchise operation that sells rights to specific territories or product lines to others. Each will require further legal, financial and marketing research.

Management Plan

Who will do what?

Be sure to include four basic sets of information:

1. State a personal history of principals and related work, hobby or volunteer experience (include formal resumes in Appendix)

2. List and describe specific duties and responsibilities of each

3. List benefits and other forms of compensation for each

4. Identify other professional resources available to the business: Example: Accountant, lawyer, insurance broker, banker. Describe relationship of each to business: Example "Accountant available on part-time hourly basis, as needed, initial agreement calls for services not to exceed x hours per month at $xx.xx per hour."

To make this section graphically clear, start with a simple organizational chart that lists specific tasks and shows, *who* (type of person is more important than an individual name other than for principals) will do *what* indicate by arrows, work flow and lines of responsibility and/or communications. Consider the following examples:

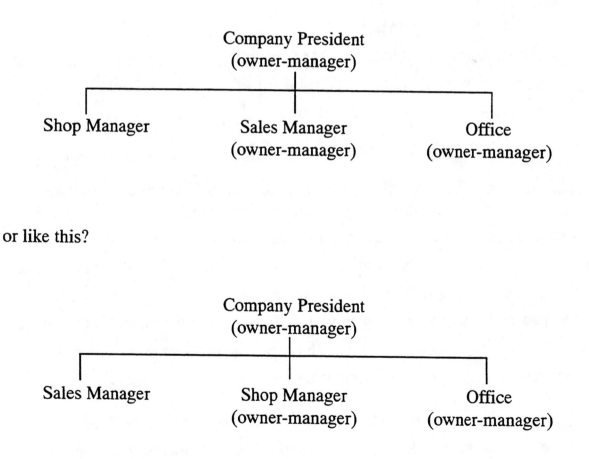

or like this?

As the service business grows, its organization chart could look like this:

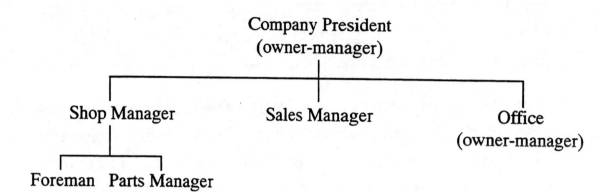

The Financial Plan

Clearly the most critical section of your business plan document is the financial plan. In formulating this part of the planning document, you will establish vital schedules that will guide the financial health of your business through the troubled waters of the first year and beyond.

Before going into the details of building the financial plan, it is important to realize that some basic knowledge of accounting is essential to the productive management of your business. If you are like most business owners, you probably have a deep and abiding interest in the product or services that you sell or intend to sell. You like to do what you do, and it is even more fulfilling that you are making money doing it. There is nothing wrong with that. Your conviction that what you are doing or making is worthwhile is vitally important to success. Nonetheless, the income of a coach who takes the greatest pride in producing a winning team will largely depend on someone keeping score of the wins and losses.

The business owner is no different. Your product or service may improve the condition of mankind for generations to come, but, unless you have access to an unlimited bankroll, you will fail if you don't make a profit. If you don't know what's going on in your business, you are not in a very good position to assure its profitability.

Most Bed & Breakfast businesses will use the "cash" method of accounting with a system of record keeping that may be little more than a carefully annotated checkbook in which is recorded all receipts and all expenditures, backed up by a few forms of original entry (invoices, receipts, cash tickets). For a Sole Partnership, the business form assumed by this Management Aid, the very minimum of recorded information is that required to accurately complete the Federal Internal Revenue Service Form 1040, Schedule C. Other business types (partnerships, joint ventures, corporations) have similar requirements but use different tax forms.

If your business is, or will be, larger than just a small supplement to family income, you will need something more sophisticated. Stationery stores can provide you with several packaged small business account systems complete with simple journals and ledgers and detailed instructions in understandable language.

Should you feel that your accounting knowledge is so rudimentary that you will need professional assistance to establish your accounting system, the classified section of your telephone directory can lead you to a number of small business services that offer a complete range of accounting services. You can buy as much as you need, from a simple "pegboard" system all the way to computerized accounting, tax return service and monthly profitability consultation. Rates are reasonable for the services rendered and an investigative consultation will usually be free. Look under the heading, "Business Consultants," and make some calls.

Let's start by looking at the makeup of the financial plan for the business.

The Financial plan includes the following:

1. Financial Planning Assumptions - these are short statements of the conditions under which you plan to operate.

- Market health
- Date of start-up
- Sales build-up ($)
- Gross profit margin
- Equipment, furniture and fixtures required
- Payroll and other key expenses that will impact the financial plan

2. Operations Plan - Profit and Loss Projection - this is prepared for the first year's Budget. Appendix A-11.

3. Source of Funds Schedule - this shows the source(s) of your funds to capitalize the business and how they will be distributed among your fixed assets and working capital.

4. Pro Forma Balance Sheet - "Pro forma" refers to the fact that the balance sheet is before the fact, not actual. This form displays Assets, Liabilities and Equity of the business. This will indicate how much Investment will be required by the business and how much of it will be used as Working Capital in its operation.

5. Cash Flow Projection - this will forecast the flow of cash into and out of your business through the year. It helps you plan for staged purchasing, high volume months and slow periods.

Creating the Profit and Loss Projection.

Appendix A-11. Create a wide sheet of analysis paper with a three inch wide column at the extreme left and thirteen narrow columns across the page. Write at the top of the first page the planned name of your business. On the second line of the heading, write "Profit and Loss Projection." On the third line, write "First Year."

Then, note the headings on Appendix A-11 and copy them onto your 12-column sheet, copy the headings from the similar area on Exhibit A. Then follow the example set by Appendix A-11 and list all of the other components of your income, cost and expense structure. You may add or delete specific loans of expense to suit your business plan. Guard against consolidating too many types of expenses under one account lest you lose control of the components. At the same time, don't try to break down expenses so discretely that accounting becomes a nuisance instead of a management tool. Once again, Exhibit A provides ample detail for most businesses.

Now, in the small column just to the left of the first monthly column, you will want to note which of the items in the left-hand column are to be estimated on a monthly (M) or yearly (Y) basis. Items such as Sales, Cost of Sales and Variable expenses will be estimated monthly based on planned volume and seasonal or other estimated fluctuations. Fixed Expenses can usually be estimated on a yearly basis and divided by twelve to arrive at even monthly values. The "M" and "Y" designations will be used later to distinguish between variable and fixed expense.

Depreciation allowances for Fixed Assets such as production equipment, office furniture and machines, vehicles, etc. will be calculated from the Source of Funds Schedule.

Appendix A-11 describes line by line how the values on the Profit and Loss Projection are developed. Use this as your guide.

Source of Funds Schedule
To create this schedule, you will need to create a list of all the Assets that you intend to use in your business, how much investment each will require and the source of funds to capitalize them. A sample of such a list is shown below:

Asset	Cost	Source of Funds
Cash	$2,500	Personal savings
Accounts Receivable	3,000	From profits
Inventory	2,000	Vendor credit
Pickup truck	5,000	Currently owned
Packaging machine	10,000	Installment purchase
Office desk and chair	300	Currently owned
Calculator	75	Personal cash
Electric typewriter*	500	Personal savings

*   A note about office equipment, test use or rent two or more brands that appear to meet your needs and select the one with which you feel most comfortable. Don't be afraid to ask others who have had to make this decision for advice. Compatibility of your system with those of potential typesetting services or printers should be of high considerations. If you are not quite sure, consider renting or leasing the equipment until you are. Service contracts on such complex electronic gear are usually a good insurance policy.

Before you leave your Source of Funds Schedule, indicate the number of months (years x 12) of useful life for depreciable fixed assets. (An example, the pickup truck, the packaging machine and the furniture and office equipment would be depreciable.) Generally, any individual item of equipment, furniture, fixtures, vehicles, etc., costing over $100 should be depreciated. For more information on allowances for depreciation, you can get free publications and assistance from your local Internal Revenue Service office. Divided the cost of each fixed asset item by the number or months over which it will be depreciated. You will need this data to enter as monthly depreciation on your Profit and Loss Projection. All of the data on the Source of Funds Schedule will be needed to create the Balance Sheet.

Creating the Pro Forma Balance Sheet

Appendix A-13. This is the Balance Sheet Form. There are a number of variations of this form and you may find it prudent to ask your banker for the form that the bank uses for small business. It will make it easier for them to evaluate the health of your business. Use this to get started and transfer the data to your preferred form later. Accompanying Appendix A-12 which describes line by line how to develop the Balance Sheet.

Even though you may plan to stage the purchase of some assets through the year, for the purpose of this pro forma Balance Sheet, assume that all assets will be provided at the start-up.

Cash Flow Projection

An important subsidiary schedule to your financial plan is a monthly Cash Flow Projection. Prudent business management practice is to keep no more cash in the business than is needed to operate it and to protect it from catastrophe. In most small businesses, the problem is rarely one of having too much cash. A Cash Flow Projection is made to advise management of the amount of cash that is going to be absorbed by the operation of the business and compares it against the amount that will be available.

SBA has created an excellent form for this purpose and it is shown as Appendix B. Your projection should be prepared on 13-column analysis paper to allow for a twelve-month projection. Appendix B represents a line by line description and explanation of the components of the Cash Flow Projection which provides a step-by-step method of preparation.

Resources

U.S. Small Business Administration
Office of Business Development

Business Development Publication
MP15

Bed & Breakfast
Business Associations for the Entrepreneur

American Bed and Breakfast Association (ABBA)
10800 Midlothian Tpke
Richmond, VA 23235-4700
Sarah Sonke, Dir.
PH: (804) 379-2222   TF: (800) 769-2468
FX: (804) 379-1469
Founded: 1982   Members: 600

Bed and Breakfast League/Sweet Dreams and Toast (BBL)
P.O. Box 9490
Washington, DC 20016
Millie Grooby, Dir.
PH: (202) 363-7767
Founded: 1976

NationalBed and Breakfast Association (NB&BA)
P.O. Box 332
Norwalk, CT 06852
Phyllis Featherton, Pres.
PH: (202) 847-6196   FX: (202) 847-6510
Founded: 1980   Members: 2,000

Notes

Chapter 7

Managing The Business

Delegating work, responsibility, and authority is difficult in a small business because it means letting others make decisions which involved spending the owner/manager's money. At a minimum, he should delegate enough authority to get the work done, to allow assistants to take initiative, and to keep the operation moving in his absence. Coaching those who carry responsibility and authority in self-improvement is essential and emphasis in allowing competent assistants to perform in their own style rather than insisting that things be done exactly as the owner/manager would personally do them is important. "Let others take care of the details" is the meaning of delegating work and responsibility. In theory, the same principles for getting work done through other people apply whether you have 25 employees and one top assistant or 150 to 200 employees and several keymen yet, putting the principles into practice is often difficult.

Delegation is perhaps the hardest job owner/managers have to learn. Some never do. They insist on handling many details and work themselves into early graves. Others pay lip service to the idea but actually run a one-man shop. They give their assistants many responsibilities but little or no authority. Authority is the fuel that makes the machine go when you delegate word and responsibility. If an owner/manager is to run a successful company, he must delegate authority properly. How much authority is proper depends on your situation. At a minimum, you should delegate enough authority: (1) to get the work done, (2) to allow keymen to take initiative, (3) to keep things going in your absence.

The person who fills a key management spot in the organization must either be a manager or be capable of becoming one. A manager's chief job is to plan, direct, and coordinate the work of others. He should possess the three "I's" — Initiative, Interest, and Imagination. The manager of a department must have enough self-drive to start and keep things moving. Personality traits must be considered. A keyman should be strong-willed enough to overcome opposition when necessary.

When you manage through others, it is essential that you keep control. You do it by holding a subordinate responsible for his actions and checking the results of those actions. In controlling your assistants, try to strike a balance. You should not get into a keyman's operations so closely that you are "in his hair" nor should you be so far removed that you lose control of things.

You need feedback to keep yourself informed. Reports provide a way to get the right kind of feedback at the right time. This can be daily, weekly, or monthly depending on how soon you need the information. Each department head can report his progress, or lack of it, in the unit of production that is appropriate for his activity; for example, items packed in the shipping room, sales per territory, hours of work per employee.

For the owner/manager, delegation does not end with good control. It involves coaching as well, because management ability is not required automatically. You have to teach it. Just as important, you have to keep your managers informed just as you would be if you were doing their jobs.

Part of your job is to see that they get the facts they need for making their decisions. You should be certain that you convey your thinking when you coach your assistants. Sometimes words can be inconsistent with thoughts. Ask questions to make sure that the listener understands your meaning. In other words, delegation can only be effective when you have good communications.

Sometimes an owner/manager finds himself involved in many operational details even though he does everything that is necessary for delegation of responsibility. In spite of defining authority, delegation, keeping control, and coaching, he is still burdened with detailed work. Usually, he had failed to do one vital thing. He has refused to stand back and let the wheels turn.

If the owner/manager is to make delegation work, he must allow his subordinates freedom to do things their way. He and the company are in trouble if he tries to measure his assistants by whether they do a particular task exactly as he would do it. They should be judged by their results — not their methods. No two persons react exactly the same in every situation. Be prepared to see some action taken differently from the way in which you would do it even though your policies are well defined. Of course, if an assistant strays too far from policy, you need to bring him back in line. You cannot afford second-guessing.

You should also keep in mind that when an owner/manager second-guesses his assistants, he risks destroying their self-confidence. If the assistant does not run his department to your satisfaction and if his shortcomings cannot be overcome, then replace him. But when results prove his effectiveness, it is good practice to avoid picking at each move he makes.

Notes

Chapter 8

Business Resource Information

Books

Steps To: Small Business Start-up,
 by Linda Pinson and Jerry Jinnett (Kaplan Publishing, 2006).

Blue's Clues for Success: The 8 Secrets Behind a Phenomenal Business,
 by Diane Tracy (Dearborn, 2001).

Entrepreneur Magazine's Start Your Own Business, 3rd. ed.,
 by Rieva Lesonsky (Entrepreneur Press, 2004).

MBA in a Day: What You Would Learn at the Top-Tier Business Schools,
 by Steven Stralser (New York: John Wiley & Sons, 2004).

Own Your Own Corporation: Why the Rich Own Their Own Companies and Everyone Else Works for them,
 by Garrett Sutton, Robert T. Kiyosaki, and Ann Blackman (Warner Books, 2001).

Portratis of Success: 9 Keys to Sustaining Value in Any Business,
 by James Olan Hutcheson (Dearborn, 2002).

Small Time Operator: How to Start Your Own Business, Keep Your Books, Pay Your Taxes, and Stay Out of Trouble, (Small Time Operator, 27th Edition)
 by Bernard B. Kamoroff, (Bell Springs Publishing, 2005).

Successful Business Planning in 30 Days: A Step-by-Step Guide for Writing a Business Plan and Starting Your Own Business,
 by Peter J. Patsula (Patsul Media, 2000).

Straight Talk About Starting and Growing Your Business,
 by Sanjyot P. Dunung (McGraw Hill, 2006).

Associations and Organizations

U.S. Department of Commerce
14th Street and Constitution Avenue NW
Room 5055
Washington, DC 20210
Phone: 202-482-5061
Web site: *rvwm.mbda.gov*

U.S. Department of Labor
200 Constitution Avenue NW
Washington, DC 20210
Web site: *www.dol.gov*

Federal Trade Commission
600 Pennsylvania Avenue NW
Washington, DC 20580
General information: 202-326-2222
Anti-trust and competition issues: 202-326-3300
Web site: *www.ftc.gov*

U.S. Small Business Administration (SBA)
403 3rd Street SW
Washington, DC 20416
Phone: 202-205-7701
Web site: *www.sba.gov*

SBA Regional Offices
- Region 1, Boston: 617-565-8415
- Region 2, New York: 212-264-1450
- Region 3, King of Prussia, PA: 215-962-3700
- Region 4, Atlanta: 404-347-995
- Region 5, Chicago: 310-353-5000
- Region 6, Ft. Worth, TX: 817-885-6581
- Region 7, Kansas City, MO: 816-374-6380
- Region 8, Denver: 303-844-0500
- Region 9, San Francisco: 415-744-2118
- Region 10, Seattle: 206-553-7310

Internal Revenue Service
Washington, DC 20224
Phone: 800429-1040
Web site: *www.irs.ustres.gov*

The IRS has an expansive Web site where you can find a great deal of tax help and a state-by-state guide for locating state tax information. There are also numerous tax publications (all numbered) including:

- Tax Guide for Small Business, Publication #334
- Self-Employment Tax, Publication #533
- Business Expenses, Publication #535

For tax forms go to *www.irs.ustres.gov/forms*

International Franchise Association
1350 New York Avenue NW
Suite 900
Washington, DC 20005-4709
Phone: 202-628-8000

American Association of Franchises and Dealers
P.O. Box 81887
San Diego, CA 92138-1887
Phone: 800-733-9858
Web site: *www.aafd.org*

Associations and Organizations

**National Association of Women
  Business Owners**
1411 K Street NW
Suite 1300
Washington, DC 20005
Phone: 202-347-8686
Fax: 202-347-4130
Information service line: 800-556-2926
Web site: *www.nawbo.org*

The National Association for the Self-Employed
1023 15 Street NW
Suite 1200
Washington, DC 20005-2600
Phone: 202-466-2100
Web site: *www.nase.com*
The NASE works to help the self-employed
make their businesses successful and provides
numerous benefits and services. It was formed
over twenty years ago by small business owners.

**Occupational Safety and Health Administra-
tion (OSHA)**
200 Constitution Avenue NW
Washington, DC 20210
Web site: *www.osha-slc.gov*

Institute For Occupational Safety and Health
Phone: 800-35-NIOSH or 513-533-8328
Web site: *www.cdc.gov/niosh*

Dun & Bradstreet
Austin, Texas 78731
Phone: 800-234-3867
Web site: *www.dnb.com*
For over 160 years, D&B has been providing
companies with information and assistance in
making key business decisions.

**American Entrepreneurs for
  Economic Growth**
1655 North Fort Myer Drive
Suite 850
Arlington, VA 22209
Phone: 703-524-3743
Web site: *www.aeeg.org*

**National Association of
  Home-Based Businesses**
10451 Mill Run Circle
Suite 400
Owings Mills, MD 21117
Phone: 410-363-3698
Web site: *www.usahomebusiness.com*

U.S. Census Bureau
Washington DC 20233
Phone: 301-457-4608
Web site: *www.census.gov*

U.S. Patent and Trademark Office
General Information Services Division
Crystal Plaza 3, Room 2CO2
Washington, DC 20231
Phone: 800-786-9199 or 703-308-4357
Web site: *www.uspto.gov*

U.S. Securities & Exchange Commission
450 Fifth Street NW
Washington, DC 20549
Office of Investor Education
  and Assistance: 202-942-7040
Web site: *www.sec.gov*

Associations and Organizations

**American Association of
   Home Based Businesses**
Fax: 301-963-7042
P.O. Box 10023
Rockville, MD 20849
Website: *www.aahbb.org*

American Small Businesses Association
800-942-2722
8773 IL Route 75E
Rock City, IL 61070

Home Business Institute
561-865-0865
P.O. Box 480215
Delray Beach, FL 33448
Website: *www.hbiweb.com*

Marketing Research Association
860-257-4008
1344 Silas Deane Highway, Suite 306,
Rocky Hill, CT 06067
Website: *www.mra-net.org*

**National Association of the
   Self-Employed (NASE)**
800-252-NASE (800-232-6273)
P.O. Box 612067
DFW Airport
Dallas, TX 75261-2067
Website: *www.nase.org*

Magazines

Entrepreneur Magazine, Business Start-Ups Magazine, and **Entrepreneur's Home Office**
Entrepreneur Media, Inc.
2392 Morse Avenue
Irvine, CA 92614
Phone: 714-261-2325
Web site: *www.entrepreneurmag.com*

Forbes
60 Fifth Avenue
New York, NY 10011
Phone: 212-620-2200
Web site: *www.forbes.com*

Inc. Magazine
38 Commercial Wharf
Boston, MA 02110
Phone: 617-248-8000 or 800-2340999
Web site: *www.inc.com*

My Business Magazine
Hammock Publishing, Inc.
3322 West End Avenue
Suite 700
Nashville, TN 37203
Phone: 615-385-9745

Consumer Goods Manufacturer
Edgell Communications
10 West Hanover Avenue
Suite 107
Randolph, NJ 07869

Minority Business Entrepreneur
3528 Torrance Boulevard
Suite 101
Torrance, CA 90503
Phone: 310-540-9398
Web site: *www.mbemag.com*

Workforce ACC Communications
245 Fischer Avenue
Suite B-2
Costa Mesa, CA 92626
Phone: 714-751-4106
Web site: *www.workforceonline.com*

Websites

www.allbusiness.com
A comprehensive site with resources for small and medium sized businesses.

www.bizweb.com
A guide to some 47,000 companies.

www.bplan.com
Numerous sample business plans for various industries.

www.bspage.com
The Business Start page includes a short course on starting a business, tips, and reviews of top business books.

www.business.gov
The U.S. Business Advisor is a one-stop shop for working with the many government agencies that impact upon business.

www.businessfinance. com
A major online source for finding potential investors.

www.businessnation.com
Business news, a library, discussions, opportunities, and resources.

www.businesstown.com
Information and articles from starting to selling your business.

www.catalogconsultancy.com
Information and guidance for catalog and direct mail businesses.

www.chamber-of-commerce.com
Links to local chamber of commerce Web sites, and e-mail addresses.

www.financenet.com
Sponsored by the US Chief Financial Officers Council, FinanceNet has a wealth of information and resources available specializing in public financial management.

www.globalbizdirectory.com
Massive director of retail, agricultural, mining, and numerous other business-related organizations and associations. Includes a state-by-state and international listing database.

www.gomez.com
Gomez offers business new and detailed report cards and consumer responses on e-commerce Web sites in various sectors.

www.homebusiness.com
Detailed information and business solutions for the home base business.

www.hoovers.com
Provides detailed business and company information, industry report links, professional help, business news, and more.

www.ideacafe.com
A good place for news, tips, expert advice ideas, and schmoozing with other small business owners.

www.inc.com
A wealth of articles and advice about starting and growing your business from the folks at Inc. Magazine.

www.marketingsource.com/associations
Find any association in any industry at this valuable resource site.

www.morebusiness.com
Articles, tips, sample business and marketing plans, legal forms contracts, a newsletter, and more offered for entrepreneurs.

www.nasbic.org
The National Association of Small Business Investment Companies promotes growth in the business sector through numerous programs.

Library Resources

Almanac of Business and Industrial Financial Ratios
(Prentice-Hall). Provides ratios and industry norms in actual dollar figures derived from IRS data. Each industry includes performance indicators such as total assets, cost of operations, wages, and profit margins.

American Wholesaler and Distributor Directory
(Gale Research). Provides listings of wholesalers and distributors sorted by product category and state.

Catalog of Catalogs
(Woodbine House). Contains descriptions and contact information for more than 14,000 catalogs, indexed by subject and company name.

Directory of Manufacturers' Sales Agencies
(Manufacturing Agents National Association). Lists manufacturers' sales agencies alphabetically and by state. Also has information on how to select a sales agent.

Encyclopedia of Associations
(Gale Research). Guise to national and international associations; contains contact information and descriptions; indexed by name, key word, and geographic area.

Financial Studies of the Small Business
(Financial Research Associates). Organized by industry; contains financial ratios and indicators for small and microbusinesses.

Lifestyle Market Analyst
(Standard Rate & Data Service). Reference book containing demographic and psychographic statistics for metropolitan statistical areas in the United States.

Small business Profiles
(Gale Research). Contains sources of information related to starting specific types of small businesses. Typical entries include start-up information, trade associations and publications, statistics, and supply sources.

Thomas Food Industry Register.
Directory of food manufacturers and suppliers to the food industry.

Thomas Register of Manufacturing.
Directory of most manufacturing firms; includes company profile and contact information.

The Small Business Administration

The U.S. Small Business Administration was established in 1953 to provide financial, technical, and management assistance to entrepreneurs. Statistics show that most small business failures are due to poor management. For this reason, the SBA places special emphasis on business management training that covers such topics as planning, finance, organization, and marketing. Often, training is held in cooperation with educational institutions, chambers of commerce, and trade associations. Prebusiness workshops are held on a regular basis for prospective business owners. Other training programs are conducted that focus on special needs such as rural development and international trade. One-on-one counseling is provided through the Service Corps of Retired Executives (SCORE) and Small Business Development Centers (SBDC). The SBA strives to match the needs of a specific business with the expertise available.

To access the SBA: Online http://www.sba.gov
                     SBA Answer Desk 800-827-5722

SCORE is a volunteer program that helps small business owners solve their operating problems through free one-on-one counseling and through a well-developed system of low-cost workshops and training sessions. To located a SCORE counseling center in your area or to consult online, access the following site: http://www.score.org
SBDCs are generally located or headquartered in academic institutions and provide individual counseling and practical training for prospective and current business owners. To locate a center near you, log on to http://www.sba.gov/sbdc.

A Concise Guide To Starting Your Own Business

Page A-2

Guide Overview

A concise overview of the complete guide to starting and operating a successful business.

The following topics are presented:

- Business Plan for Small Businesses.
- Getting Started
- Deciding Where To Start The Business
- Business Patronage Statistics
- Site Location
- Site Selection Criteria — Some General Questions.
- Choosing The Proper Method of Organization
- What Is A Corporation?
- Estimating Start-up Costs
- Preparing An Income Statement
- Preparing A Balance Sheet
- Marketing The Business
- Marketing Planning — An Outline for Marketing
- Advertising Media
- Management and Getting The Work Done
- Sample Organization Chart
- Summary of the Business Plan
- Guide Summary
- Reference Materials

Business Plan for Small Businesses

Page A-4

Getting Started

Following is a list of what you need to accomplish to insure that your business endeavor will head in the right direction.

1. Define your educational background and work experience
2. Survey all basic types of businesses.
3. Define what type of business matches your experience and educational background.
4. Choose only the business that you would like to own and operate.
5. Define what products or services your business will be marketing.
6. Define who will be using your products/services.
7. Define why they will be purchasing your products/services.
8. List all competitors in your marketing area.

Deciding Where to Start the Business

Will your business fulfill a need in the area you plan to bring your business to? This section provides you with some important information you need to examine before taking your ideas any further:

1. Decide where you want to live.
2. Choose several areas that would match your priorities.
3. Use the list that follows as a guide to see if your location will match the estimated population needed to support your business. The numbers which follow the type of business indicate the typical number of inhabitants per year.

Business Patronage Statistics

Food Stores
Grocery Stores 1,534
Meat and Fish
    (Sea Food) Markets . . . 17,876
Candy, Nut, and
    Confectionery Stores . . 31,409
Retail Bakeries 12,563
Dairy Products Stores . . . 41,587

Eating and Drinking
Restaurant, Lunch Rooms . 1,583
Cafeterias 19,341
Refreshment Places 3,622
Drinking Places 2,414

General Merchandise
Variety Stores 10,373
General Merchandise 9,837

Apparel/Accessories Stores
Women's Ready-To-
    Wear Stores 7,102
Women's Accessory and
    Specialty Stores 25,824
Men's and Boy's Clothing
    and Furnishings 11,832
Family Clothing 16,890
Shoe Stores 9,350

Furniture, Home Furnishings, and Equipment Stores
Furniture Stores 7,210
Floor Covering 29,543
Drapery, Curtains, and
    Upholstery Stores 62,585
House, Appliances 12,485
Radios and TV's 20,346
Record Shops 112,144
Musical Instruments 46,332

Building Materials, Hardware, and Farm Equipment Dealers
Lumber and other Building
    Materials Dealers 8,124
Paint, Glass, and Wallpaper
    Stores 22,454
Hardware Stores 10,206
Farm Equipment Dealers . 14,793

Automotive Dealers
Motor Vehicle Dealers,
    New and Used Cars 6,000
Motor Vehicle Dealers,
    Used Cars only 17,160
Tire, battery, and
    Accessory Dealers 8,800

Boat Dealers 61,500

Household Trailer Dealers . 44,746

Gasoline Service Stations . . . 1,395

Miscellaneous
Antique and Secondhand
    Stores 17,170
Book and Stationery Stores 28,580
Drugstores 4,268
Florists 13,531
Fuel Oil Dealers 25,000
Garden Supply Stores . . . 65,000
Gift, Novelty Shops 26,000
Hobby, Toy, and Game
    Shops 61,000
Jewelry Stores 13,400
Optical Goods Stores 62,800
Sporting Goods Store 27,000

From *Starting and Managing a Small Business of Your Own, 1973;*
Small Business Administration, Washington, DC

Page A-6

Site Location

1. Define your number of inhabitants per store.

2. Locate several sites/locations that will match your inhabitants per stores.

3. Define population and its growth potential.

4. Define local ordinances and zoning regulations that you will need in order to start your type of business.

5. Define your trading area and all competitors in your trading area.

6. Define parking need, for your kind of business.

7. Define special needs, etc., lighting, heating, ventilation.

8. Define rental cost of site/location.

9. Define why customers will come to your site/location.

10. Define the future of your site/location as to population growth.

11. Define your space needs and match with site/location selection.

12. Define the image of your business and make sure it matches your site/location.

Site Selection Criteria — Some General Questions

- Is the site centrally located to reach my market?

- What is the transportation availability and what are the rates?

- What provisions for future expansion can I make:

- What is the topography of the site (slope and foundation)?

- What is the housing availability for workers and managers?

- What environmental factors (schools, cultural, community atmosphere) might affect my business and my employees?

- What will the quality of this site be in 5 years, 10 years, 25 years?

- What is my estimate of this site in relation to my major competitor?

- What other media are available for advertising? How many radio and television stations are there?

- Is the Quantity and quality of available labor concentrated in a given area in the city or town? If so, is commuting a way of living in that city or town?

- Is the city centrally located to my suppliers?

- What are the labor conditions, including such things as relationships with the business community and average wages and salaries paid?

- Is the local business climate healthy, or are business failures especially high in the area?

- What about tax requirements? Is there a city business tax? Income tax? What is the property tax rate? Is there a personal property tax? Are there other special taxes?

- Is the available police and fire protection adequate?

- Is the city or town basically well planned and managed in terms of such items as electric power, sewage, and paved streets and sidewalks?

Page A-8

Choosing the Proper Method of Organization

Listed below are legal forms of business available to the small business entrepreneur:

Sole Proprietorship

Advantages
- Simple to start
- All profits to owner
- Owner in direct control
- Easy entry and exit
- Taxed as individual

Disadvantages
- Unlimited liability
- "Jack-of-all-trades"
- Capital requirement limited
- Limited life
- Employee turn-over

Partnership

Advantages
- Easy to originate
- Credit rating
- Talent combination
- Legal Contract

Disadvantages
- Unlimited liability
- Misunderstandings
- Partner withdrawal
- Regulations

Corporation

Advantages
- Limited liability
- Expansion potential
- Transfer of ownership
- Retain employees

Disadvantages
- Double taxation
- Charter restrictions
- Employee motivation
- Legal regulations

What Is A Corporation?

A corporation is an artificial being, invisible, intangible, and existing only in contemplation of the law," wrote Chief Justice John Marshall. In other words, the corporation exists as a separate entity apart from its owners, the shareholders. It makes contracts; it is liable; it pays taxes. It is a "legal person".

The corporation is the most complex of the three major forms of business ownership. The corporation stands as a separate legal entity in the eyes of the law. The life of the corporation is independent of the owners' lives. Because the owners, called shareholders, are legally separate from the corporation, they can sell their interests in the business without affecting the continuation of the business. When a corporation is founded, it accepts the regulations and restrictions placed on it by the state in which it is incorporated and any other state in which it chooses to do business. Generally, the corporation must report its financial operations to the state's attorney general on an annual basis.

Estimating Start-up Costs

Item	Amount
Fixtures and Equipment	$ _____
Building & Land (If Needed)	_____
Store and/or Office Supplies	_____
Remodeling and Decorating	_____
Deposits on Utilities	_____
Insurance	_____
Installation of Fixtures	_____
Legal Fees	_____
Professional Fees	_____
Telephone	_____
Rental	_____
Salaries and Wages	_____
Inventory if Retailing	_____
Licenses and Permits	_____
Advertising and Promotion	_____
TOTAL Estimated Start-up Cost	$ _____

Preparing An Income Statement

What is an Income Statement?

The income statement shows the income received and the expenses incurred over a period of time. Income received (sales) comes essentially from the sales of the merchandise or service which your business is formed to sell. Expenses incurred are the expired costs that have been incurred during the same period of time.

Plan A Budgeted Income Statement For One Year

1. Project Total Sales
2. Estimate Total Expenditures
3. Example Listed Below for Income Statement

Percents	1	2	3	4	5	6	7	8	9	10	11	12
Sales												
Cost of Sales												
Gross Profit												
Expenditure												
Rent Expense												
Supplies												
Wages/Salaries												
Utilities												
Insurance												
Depreciation												
Interest												
Miscellaneous												
Net Profit												

Preparing A Balance Sheet

What is a Balance Sheet?

The balance sheet shows the assets, liabilities and owner's net worth in a business as of a given date.

- Assets are the things owned by your business, including both physical things and claims against others.
- Liabilities are the amounts owned to others, the creditors of the firm.
- Net worth or owner's equity is the owner's claim to the assets after liabilities are accounted for.

A Budgeted Balance Sheet For One Year

- List all your business property at their cost to you: these are your assets.
- List all debts, or what your business owes on all your property; these are your liabilities.
- Take your total property balance (Assets), and subtract the total amount you owe (Liabilities).
- The balance is what you own in your business called (Owner's equity).
- Add Total Liabilities (2) & Total Owner's Equity (3).
- Listed on the next page is an example of a balance sheet.

NAME OF BUSINESS
BALANCE SHEET
DATE

ASSETS
Current Assets
  Cash
  Accounts Receivable   _____
Merchandise Inventories   _____
    TOTAL CURRENT ASSETS   _____
                          _____

Fixed Assets
  Land
  Building   _____
  Equipment   _____
    TOTAL FIXED ASSETS   _____
      TOTAL ASSETS   _____   1). _____

LIABILITIES
Current Liabilities
  Accounts Payable
  Note Payable   _____
  Payroll Taxes Payable   _____
    TOTAL CURRENT LIABILITIES   _____

Long-term Liabilities
  Mortgage Payable
  Long-term Note   _____
    TOTAL LONG-TERM LIABILITIES   _____
      TOTAL LIABILITIES   _____   2). _____

OWNER'S EQUITY
Proprietor's Capital   3). _____

      TOTAL LIABILITIES & OWNER'S EQUITY   (2 & 3). _____

Marketing The Business

1. Define Your Market
   • Type of Customers
   • Age, Income, Occupation of your customers
   • Type of Trading Area

2. Promotion of Your Business
   • Advertising
   • Setting your Image

3. Customer Policy Plan
   • Develop a Customer Profile
   • Customer Services
   • Customer Needs

4. Pricing Your Products/Services
   • Know all your Costs
   • Know your Profit Margin
   • Know Competitor's Price
   • Know what Return you want on your Investment

5. Sales Promotion
   • Coupons   • Demonstrations
   • Contests   • Giveaways
   • Displays   • Banners

6. Public Relations
   • Newspaper Article   • Radio Promotion
   • Contact Trade Association • TV Promotion

7. Segmentation of your Market
   • Age   • Location
   • Occupation   • Education
   • Income   • Hobbies

Marketing Planning

Outline for Marketing

I. Product/Service Concept:
    a. Name of product or service
    b. Descriptive characteristics of product or service
    c. Unit sales
    d. Analysis of market trends

II. Number of Customers in your Market Area:
    a. Profile of customers
    b. Average customer expenditure
    c. Total market

III. Your Market Potential:
    a. Total market divided by competition
    b. Total market multiplied by percent who will buy your product

IV. Needs of Customers:
    a. Identification
    b. Pleasure
    c. Social approval
    d. Personal interest
    e. Price

V. Direct Marketing Sources:
    a. Trade magazines
    b. Trade associations
    c. Small Business Administration (SBA)
    d. Government Publications
    e. Yellow pages
    f. Marketing directories

VI Customer Profile:
    a. Geographical
    b. Gender
    c. Age range
    d. Income brackets
    e. Occupation
    f. Educational level

Advertising Media

Medium	Market Coverage	Type of Audience
Daily newspaper	Single community or entire metro area: zoned editions sometimes available	General
Weekly newspaper	Single Community	Residents
Telephone Directory	Geographical area or occupational field served by the directory	Active shoppers for goods or services
Direct mail audience	Controlled by the advertiser	Controlled
Radio audience	Definable market area	Selected
Television audience	Definable market area surrounding TV Stations	Various
Outdoor	Entire metro area	General auto drivers
Magazine	Entire metro area or magazine region	Selected audience

Management and Getting the Work Done

1. Define your objective for starting your business.

2. Define your goals: profit growth for first three years.

3. Develop an organization chart of your business.

4. Define your personal needs.
   • Hiring proper employees
   • Training employees
   • Motivation

5. Define all responsibility for each person in your business.

6. Define all authority.
   • Who will hire and fire?
   • Who will select and train all personnel?
   • Who will keep the important records as to inventory, purchasing, sales records, cash records, etc.?

7. Define all laws and regulations that will be requirements for operating your business.

8. Review all duties and tasks with all your employees.

9. Write a summary of all the important tasks that you want to finish in your first year in business.

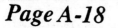

Sample Organization Chart

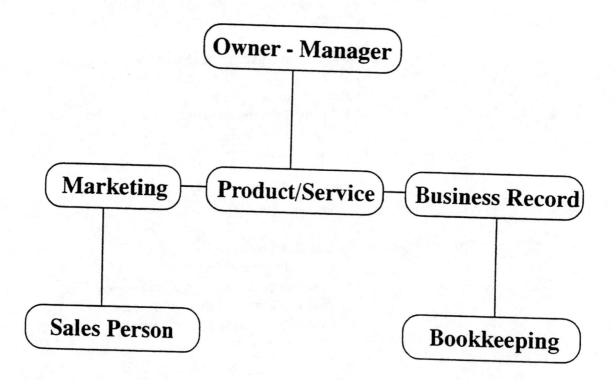

Summary of The Business Plan

Name of Business
BUSINESS PLAN
Date

1. Define your business
   - Name all principals
   - Address and phone number

2. Define your products or services

3. Define your market

4. Define your site or location

5. Advertising Plan
   - Budget
   - Media

6. Chart of Start-up cost

7. Worksheet of Income Statement
   - Revenue/Income
   - Expenses

8. Worksheet of Balance Sheet
   - Assets (Property)
   - Capital (Owner's Equity)
   - Liabilities (Debts)

9. Personnel Outline
   - Number of Employees
   - Staffing & Training

10. Management Organization
    - Organization Chart
    - Evaluation Policy
    - Job Profile

11. Special Statement
    - 3-Year Sales Schedule
    - Cash Flow
    - 3-Year Expense Schedule

Appendix A Summary

1. Contact your State Commerce Department for guidelines in starting your business.

2. Contact your City/County Clerk for guidelines in starting your business.

3. Contact all other Governmental Centers that will furnish you all the legal regulations and tax laws that will effect your business.
   - State Government
   - Internal Revenue Service
   - State Employment Security Commission
   - Department of Treasury
   - City Governmental Units

     a. Fire
     b. Police
     c. Zoning
     d. Building Permits
     e. Health
     f. Water & Sewage

4. Township Government
   - Local Legal Requirements
   - Local Taxes
   - Local Health Permits
   - Local Zoning Laws

Reference Materials

Management Aids Titles

Contact the

**Small Business Administration
P.O. Box 15434
Fort Worth, TX 76119**

for the following booklets:

- Number 2.025   Thinking About Going Into Business
- Number 2.010   Planning and Goal Setting For Business
- Number 1.016   Sound Cash Management
- Number 1.001   The A.B.C's. of Borrowing
- Number 1.008   Break-even Analysis
- Number 2.022   Business Plan For Service Firms
- Number 2.023   Business Plans for Retail Firms

Notes _____

Appendix B

HOUSEHOLD NEEDS

Many small business start-ups fail due to their inability to support their owners. Rarely do new businesses support their owners from the start. However, many individuals fail to recognize this fact. In addition, then, to a sound business plan, it is necessary for an owner to project the household cash needs month-by-month for the first three years of the business' operation. As a new business owner, you should be able to support yourself until your new business is able to support you in a manner to which you are accustomed.

MONTHLY HOUSEHOLD CASH NEEDS

Regular NON-BUSINESS Income
Spouse's salary _____
Investment income _____
Social security _____
Other income _____
Retirement benefits _____
Less taxes _____
Net monthly income _____

Regular Monthly Expenses

Housing
    Mortgage/Rent _____
    Utilities _____
    Homeowner's insurance _____
    Property taxes _____
    Home repairs _____

Living Expenses
    Groceries _____
    Telephone _____
    Tuition _____
    Transportation _____
    Meals _____
    Child care _____
    Medical expenses _____
    Clothing _____
    Personal _____

Insurance Premiums
    Life insurance _____
    Disability insurance _____
    Auto insurance _____
    Medical insurance _____

Debt Repayment
    Auto loans _____
    Consumer debt _____

Discretionary Expenses
    Entertainment _____
    Vacation _____
    Gifts _____
    Retirement contributions _____
    Investment savings _____
    Charitable contributions _____
    Dues, magazines, etc. _____
    Professional fees _____
    Other _____

Total Monthly Expenses _____

Monthly Surplus/Deficit _____

Total Year Surplus/Deficit _____
    (Monthly x 12)

Available Assets to Cover Deficit
    Checking accounts _____
    Savings accounts _____
    Money market accounts _____
    Personal credit lines _____
    Marketable securities _____
    Lump-sum retirement/
      severance _____
    Other assets _____

Total Assets _____

NEEDED RESERVES
    Total Assets-Deficit _____

PERSONAL FINANCIAL STATEMENT

This is a picture of your personal financial condition to date. It is a very important part of any loan application and/or interview, especially when a loan for a projected new business is under consideration.

PERSONAL FINANCIAL STATEMENT

_____ _____ , 19 _____

Assets
Cash
Savings accounts   _____
Stocks, bonds, other securities   _____
Accounts/Notes receivable   _____
Life insurance cash value   _____
Rebates/Refunds   _____
Autos/Other vehicles   _____
Real estate   _____
Vested pension plan/Retirement accounts   _____
Other assets   _____
                                        TOTAL ASSETS $ _____

Liabilities

Accounts payable
Contracts payable   _____
Notes payable   _____
Taxes   _____
Real estate loans   _____
Other liabilities   _____
                                   TOTAL LIABILITIES $ _____

TOTAL ASSETS $ _____

LESS TOTAL LIABILITIES $ _____

                              NET WORTH $ _____

BALANCE SHEET

A balance sheet is a current financial statement. It is a dollars and cents description of your business (existing or projected) which lists all of its assets and liabilities.

BALANCE SHEET

_____ _____ , 19 _____

	YEAR 1	YEAR II
Current Assets		
Cash	_____	_____
Accounts receivable	_____	_____
Inventory	_____	_____
Fixed Assets		
Real estate	_____	_____
Fixtures and equipment	_____	_____
Vehicles	_____	_____
Other Assets		
License	_____	_____
Goodwill	_____	_____
TOTAL ASSETS	$_____	$_____
Current Liabilities		
Notes payable (due within 1 year)	$_____	$_____
Accounts payable	_____	_____
Accrued expenses	_____	_____
Taxes owed	_____	_____
Long-Term Liabilities		
Notes payable (due after 1 year)	_____	_____
Other	_____	_____
TOTAL LIABILITIES	$_____	$_____
NETWORTH (ASSETS minus LIABILITIES)	$_____	$_____

TOTAL LIABILITIES plus NET WORTH should equal ASSETS

PROFIT AND LOSS STATEMENT

A profit and loss statement is a detailed earnings statement for the previous full year (if you are already in business). Existing businesses are also required to show a profit and loss statement for the current period to the date of the balance sheet.

PROJECTED PROFIT AND LOSS STATEMENT

	Month 1	Month 2	Month 3	Month 4	Month 5	Month 6	Month 7	Month 8	Month 9	Month 10	Month 11	Month 12
Total Net Sales												
Cost of Sales												
GROSS PROFIT												
Controllable Expenses												
Salaries												
Payroll taxes												
Security												
Advertising												
Automobile												
Dues and subscriptions												
Legal and accounting												
Office supplies												
Telephone												
Utilities												
Miscellaneous												
Total Controllable Expenses												
Fixed Expenses Depreciation												
Insurance												
Rent												
Taxes and licenses												
Loan payments												
Total Fixed Expenses												
TOTAL EXPENSES												
NET PROFIT (LOSS) (before taxes)												

CASH FLOW PROJECTIONS

A cash flow projection is a forcast of the cash (checks or money orders) a business anticipates receiving and disbursing during the course of a month. Well managed, the cash flow should be sufficient to meet the cash requirements for the following month.

CASH FLOW PROJECTIONS

	Start-up or prior to loan	Month 1	Month 2	Month 3	Month 4	Month 5	Month 6	Month 7	Month 8	Month 9	Month 10	Month 11	Month 12	TOTAL
Cash (beginning of month														
Cash on hand														
Cash in bank														
Cash in investments														
Total Cash														
Income (during month)														
Cash sales														
Credit sales payment														
Investment income														
Loans														
Other cash income														
Total Income														
TOTAL CASH AND INCOME														
Expenses (during month														
Inventory or new material														
Wages (including owner's)														
Taxes														
Equipment expense														
Overhead														
Selling expense														
Transportation														
Loan repayment														
Other cash expenses														
TOTAL EXPENSES														
CASH FLOW EXCESS (end of month)														
CASH FLOW CUMULATIVE (Monthly)														

Getting Down to Business...

How to Start & Manage a Bed & Breakfast Business

**An Instructional Guide
for Creating a Small Business
by Jerre G. Lewis, M.A.
and Leslie D. Renn, M.S.**

PLANNING AN INN, HOTEL, OR BED & BREAKFAST

Goal:

To assist you in planning your inn, hotel, or bed & breakfast

Objectives:

1. Describe the services, guests, and competition of an inn, hotel, or bed & breakfast.

2. List three personal qualities an innkeeper or owner might have.

3. List three things an innkeeper can do to make an inn special and make it "stand out from the crowd".

4. List two of the legal requirements you might have to consider before opening your inn, hotel/motel, or bed & breakfast.

What is an Inn?

Inns are small, independent hotels. Some people claim that hotels and motels have become more efficient, but also more impersonal and cold. They look for small hotels and inns where the manager/innkeeper will remember their names, where each room has its own style, and where the atmosphere is casual, private, and perhaps a bit elegant. Often the owner lives in the same building. Running an inn becomes a way of sharing your home with other people and making a business of it at the same time.

Is There Room for You?

As an innkeeper, you are selling comfort and hospitality — not just a place to sleep. Larger hotels/motels may be able to offer many more services and features than a small inn, but the personal touch is often lost — and missed by the guests. Guests appreciate the personal contact, which adds to their feelings of importance. Knowing that your inn has a friendly atmosphere, they probably will stop on their next trip. What is more, they will recommend your inn to their friends.

Are you the Type?

Before you rush off to see about opening an inn, stop and take a good look at yourself. Is this really the type of business you want to get into? Do you have the right skills and experiences, or do you need training in some area? Running an inn is a full-time job that demands physical strength and stamina. It demands being able to handle pressures. It requires an aggressive approach to profit making. Innkeeping is a 24-hour a day job, with no days off. You must play the roles of both host and business manager.

Experience:

You can get a lot of the experience you need to open an inn by working in a hotel or motel. If you do this, it will help you avoid many serious mistakes. Besides supervising employees (and you *will* need some help to run an inn), an innkeeper keeps records and has many daily responsibilities. You will oversee or work on the property, the grounds, and the guest rooms. You must supervise any services, such as housekeeping, breakfast and beverages, travel arrangements, and pet services.

In addition to work experience, a course in hotel administration would be helpful. Management and supervisory training is also available through home study or group study courses. Courses are offered by the Educational Institute of the American Hotel/Motel Association and through the Small Business Administration (SBA) Management Training Program.

Personal Qualities:

Even if you have the skills and experience to run an inn, you may not like it. You may not like having to deal constantly with people, even on those days when you've gotten up on the wrong side of the bed. If you run an inn out of your house, you may not like the lack of privacy that comes with having people -- your guests -- in your home.   Or you may not like the business aspects -- bookkeeping, managing employees, etc. You may prefer to be working for someone else.

Service Is the Name of the Game

People will come to your inn if you have something special to offer. Here is the list of some of the special services that some inns offer:

♦ Continental breakfast, served in the guests' rooms or in the dining room, including freshly squeezed orange juice

- An invitation to relax and enjoy free wine and hors d'oeuvres in the late afternoon with the inn staff

- Fresh cut flowers and plants in the lobbies and guests' rooms

- Complimentary robes if two guestrooms share a common bathroom

- Coffee and tea, available at all hours

- Parking service and facilities

- The uniqueness of the house's decor and architecture, and

- Arrangements for the convenience of the guests – a car, theatre tickets, a bouquet of flowers, a tour, a stenographer, or a picnic

Look at what other hotels/motels are doing and decide how you can be the "right" inn for your area and customers.

Getting People to Come Back

People who enjoy staying at your inn will come back *and* send their friends. What will help them to enjoy your inn? *Giving your guests prompt and efficient service.*

Any business that offers a service to people *must* give good service to get people to come back. Deal with any complaint, no matter how small. Rooms, beds and bathrooms should always be neat and clean. *These are the basics.*

If a guest complains or makes a request, do something about it at once. The most important thing to remember in the inn business is that these people are your guests as well as your customers. Serve your guests with a smile. You are in the hospitality business. Being thoughtful and considerate is the key to getting people to come back to you.

Legal Requirements

The legal requirements for opening and running an inn will depend on your location, the number of rooms in your inn, and the types of services you provide. Contact your local zoning department to ensure that your location is zoned for your business. There may be zoning restrictions regarding operating an inn in your neighborhood. Some cities require a business license to operate. You may have to file a "fictitious name statement" with the county in which you operate.

Since the name of the business may not include your name, this is a statement telling who the owner is. If you are going to provide your guests with some kind of food service, you will have to follow federal and state health and safety laws. If you serve alcohol you will be required to obtain a liquor license.

There are also requirements to meet if you hire employees. You will have to file with the IRS for an employer identification number (EIN). You may also need unemployment insurance, disability insurance, and/or workmen's compensation insurance, as required by federal and state laws.

Summary

Innkeeping is a risky business to get into. Make sure you have the right personality and know enough about the business and your competition before you start. You can give yourself a "competitive edge" through the special services you offer. There are many legal requirements for operating an inn, but don't let that stop you. Careful planning will help you avoid many problems.

Individual Activities

1. Make a list of the personal qualities you should have in order to open an inn, hotel/motel, or bed & breakfast.

2. List ways to gain experience and training as an innkeeper before you open your own business.

3. Think of the inns, hotels/motels, bed & breakfasts you have stayed in and describe the services they provided which made them memorable.

4. Call your state and county licensing agency to inquire about the legal aspects of opening and running an inn. Make a list of the requirements and report to the class on what you have learned.

CHOOSING A LOCATION

Goal:

To assist you in choosing a good location for your inn, hotel/motel, or bed & breakfast.

Objectives:

1. List three things to think about in deciding where to locate your inn, hotel/motel, or bed & breakfast.

2. Choose a location for your inn, hotel/motel, or bed & breakfast.

3. Decide whether your city/town would be a good location for an inn, hotel/motel, or bed & breakfast.

Your choice of locations will be one of the most important decisions you make when going into business, so think about it carefully. In this unit we will consider some of the facts you should think about when choosing a site for your inn, hotel/motel, or bed & breakfast.

You Come First

You can open up an inn in almost every kind of city, but your location must first fit your own requirements, especially if you intend to live there yourself. You have to consider weather, family and friends, your neighborhood, recreational facilities, and so on. If you are not happy living in or close to that city, you won't be happy having a business there.

Next Comes the City

What makes a particular city a good place for opening an inn? There are many things to consider -- traffic patterns, tourists, area industry, scenery, and the number of other inns, hotels/motels, and/or bed & breakfasts, but it all comes down to one thing -- having people who need you.

Many times you have to play detective before you can decide if a particular city will be a good location for you. There are people, organizations, and publications that can help you. Some ideas follow:

1. Check with the local Chamber of Commerce for the "economic profile" of the community. Is this a stable community? Is the community growing -- are many people moving into the area? What types of businesses are in the area?

2. Take a close look at the other inns in the area. Are they generally "booked," or do you see a lot of vacancy signs? How great a demand is there for rooms? Do visitors tend to stay a long time (a week) or a short time (over a weekend)? Are there "peak" seasons when these inns do most of their business, or is business fairly stable year-round?

3. You should also take a careful look at the actual and potential businesses and industries in the city. Certain companies may have many people traveling n and out of the area. Where do these business people stay?

4. Talk to other business people in the city. Talk to the people who will be your "neighbors." What do they think your chance of success is?

5. Talk to the old-timers and the newcomers in the hotel/motel and inn business, and learn all you can from them. Perhaps you can't copy success, but you can learn some of their secrets. Learn why some of them failed and why others succeeded.

6. Local, state, and national hotel and tourist organizations can give your information and direct you to other sources that can be helpful.

7. Several trade magazines and journals are written for people like you in the accommodations field. You may consider subscribing to those that will help you even before you become an innkeeper.

8. A real estate agent can give you ideas on costs of different areas and can tell you what buildings are currently for sale.

9. An architect may be able to give you advice on site selection, building design, engineering, materials, equipment, and other details in choosing the site and planning your inn.

10. The advice of an interior decorator may also be helpful. This person should have a knowledge of color and experience in design and decoration of public spaces.

All of these types of people and organizations are important to the success of your inn. You should feel free to consult them about your business plans.

GETTING MONEY TO START

All new businesses need money to start. Your own savings and loans from family and friends will probably be important sources of money to start your new business.

Where Will You Open Your Doors?

You may be lucky and already have a house you can use for your inn, hotel/motel, or bed & breakfast. If not, you'll have to buy one, and that takes a lot of money! Jerry and Lynn already had a good income. They also had friends who were willing to invest in them. They could afford to "put down" a large amount of money to buy the old Victorian house and pay for repairs and renovations. This was very helpful to them, but you may not have as much money available to you. What can you do?

Financial Arrangements

The price tag on the inn you are about to open will depend on the following:

♦ Whether or not you have to buy the building

♦ The money you need to renovate (i.e., additional plumbing, electrical fixtures, etc.) and decorate

♦ Your monthly operating expenses (i.e., salaries, supplies, etc.).

You may have to borrow money from a financial institution such as a bank, an investment company, or a building and loan association. The lender will want to know about you and your plan for the inn before lending you money. You will have to show that you are a good business risk, and will be asked for the following information:

♦ Personal background information (a resume)

♦ A description of your business, and

♦ A statement of financial need

Loans are difficult to get. Banks may lend up to half of the money you need *if* they can be convinced that your business has a good potential for success, you are competent and reliable, and you have a good business plan for repaying the loan.

Startup Costs

You must consider how much money you will need to borrow by first figuring out how much money you have on hand. Decide how much you will need to start your business, then ask the bank for the difference between these two amounts.

Let's assume you already have a house for your inn, hotel/motel, or bed & breakfast. You will not have to pay for rent space. In fact, you will actually be saving money, as you will be able to write off business expenses on your income tax form. However, you will still have a significant amount of start-up costs -- furniture, cleaning and laundry equipment, linens, soap, towels, other supplies, and, of course, food (if you plan to serve it).

Other start-up expenses might include fees to register your business and file for an Employer Identification Number from the IRS, taxes, licenses, installation of extra telephone equipment, plumbing and electrical fixtures in your house; the cost of employee salaries and benefits; office supplies (file folders, stamps, work order forms, stationery, etc.) and advertising.

You will also need some money to cover operating expenses for the first months you are in business -- until your income from guests is large enough to cover them. Operating expenses include utilities, advertising, and salaries -- expenses you will have every month just to keep your business running.

Following is a sample financial statement form that you can use to list your expected expenses and money on hand. Different lenders may use different forms.

STATEMENT OF FINANCIAL NEED	
Starting Expenses	**Money on Hand**
Salaries $	Cash on Hand $
Building Expenses $	Gifts or Personal Loans $
Repairs and Renovations	Investment by Others
Equipment and Furniture	
Food and Supplies	
Advertising	
Other	
Total:	**Total:**
Total Starting Expenses:	
Total Money on Hand:	
Total Loan Money Needed:	

Summary

When you apply for a loan to start your inn, hotel/motel, or bed & breakfast, you will need to provide a business description and a statement of financial need. A business description gives the details of your business. The exact amount of money you need to start will depend on whether you already have a house available, the changes/improvements needed in the building , your decorating plans, your equipment and supply needs, and the cash you have available. This figure will be different, depending on the accommodations and services you plan to offer your guests.

KEEPING TRACK OF SUPPLIES AND SCHEDULES

Your Supplies

Your supplies are the materials you need to provide service to your guests. Knowing what you need and keeping track of it all is not easy. You may buy enough towels, but what do you say to a guest who "just happens" to walk off with one of them? The important thing in buying supplies is to plan ahead so you don't run out of something when you need it.

What sorts of supplies will you need to run an inn? You will need office supplies, cleaning and housekeeping supplies, food, and personal items used by the guests (linens, towels, soap, bathmats, and ashtrays, just to name a few).

Then there are the special touches such as but flowers and vases. If your guests share a common bathroom, you may consider supplying them with bathrobes. Some inns also supply shower caps for their guests. There is no end to special touches and the supplies you will need to carry them out.

When you buy your supplies, don't buy "just enough." You're bound to run out of something. Buying "in depth" will help you keep a large enough supply on hand to meet the needs of your guests.

Below are some tips for buying your supply inventory:

♦ Buy in the right quantity

♦ Buy the right quality (scratchy towels don't go over very well)

♦ Buy at the best prices for you

♦ Buy from reliable suppliers who will give you the best service and prompt delivery

♦   Buy at the right time (before you run out)

The Source of All Things

When you start looking for suppliers, there are three basic things to consider:

1.   *When* you will receive the supplies.

2.   *How much* time you have to pay the bill.

3.   *The discount* you will receive for paying in cash.

Some suppliers will give you special prices if you pay them before a certain day and in cash. when you open your inn, you would be wise to buy from suppliers who are located close to you.   This way you won't have to worry about shipping costs or delivery dates. You will also be under less pressure to pre-plan your buying schedule and will be able to avoid the problems of having either too many supplies on hand (which takes up space), or too few. Keep careful records of what you have ordered and when. Your supplier will also be keeping records. This way you both can be sure that you get what you want, when you want it.

Keeping a Tight Rein on Your Supply Closet

Keeping track of the supplies on hand is important if you want to give your guests careful and efficient service. Knowing what supplies you have in stock helps you plan for what you will need to buy in the future and when. the simplest way to watch your supply needs is the "eyeball" method. Stack your supplies in piles so you can tell just by looking when you are getting low. If you are a small operation, this may be a good enough way to keep on top of things. However, this is not a very efficient way of keeping track of large numbers of items.

Another way to keep track of your inventory is actually counting the numbers of items you have on hand. A third type of inventory control system is one that your housekeeping staff can assist you with. Each time a room is cleaned, the staff can use a *checklist* to mark down exactly what is in the room and what may be missing.

Your choice of systems will depend on the size of your inn, the number of guests you can accommodate, and what is easiest for you. The important thing is to keep records so that you will know hwat you have and what you need. A good inventory control system will help your inn run smoothly.

Making Reservations for Your Guests

Many times people will plan and make reservations a long time in advance. You will have to be concerned about keeping track of your guests' reservations. It might get a little sticky if guests show up with a prepaid reservation and you've given their room away to someone else. That's where guest reservation forms come in. A reservation form will help yo uplan for your guests and kep track of their bills, payments, and deposits. Your reservation form should be as complete and foolproof as possible. You should fill out each one carefully.

Who's Going to Do It and When?

If you run your inn yourself, or with the help of a very small staff, you may not even want to bother with a work schedule -- as long as you can keep track of what is to be done, where, and when. When you finish one job, you can just o on to the next job.

Sometimes a work schedule comes in handy, particularly if you have a lot of details to take care of and if you have other people working for you. A work schedule is usualy a chart of work days and the people you have working for you. You should decide which persons will be responsible for which jobs and how long each job will take, then fill in the squares. Following is an example:

Employee	Work to be Completed	Special Requirements	Date	Time Completed	Remarks
Susan L.	Clean Rooms	Wash Windows	12/1	5 p.m.	Bruce can help
Bruce C.	Check in Supplies	---	12/1	Noon	---

As the day goes by, you can look at the schedule and who is doing what, when it should be done, and when it *is* done. Schedules will help your workers get the most work done in a day.

Summary

In this unit you were introduced to the basic steps in buying and keeping track of supplies and organizing your work. You will need some basic supplies to run your inn. It is important to find reliable suppliers and to keep track of your inventory. It is also important to be organized so you can give your guests reliable service.

SETTING PRICES

Goal:

To assist you in setting prices for rooms in your inn, hotel/motel, or bed & breakfast.

Objectives:

1. List three things to consider in setting room prices for guests.

2. Set prices for your inn, hotel/motel or bed & breakfast after being given certain "facts."

HOW PRICES ARE SET AT THE BED & BREAKFAST INN

Since their inn had to be competitive, Jerry and Lynn decided to investigate what other hotels, motels, and inns in the area were charging. Hotel/motel rates tended to range form $30 a night per person to $75 a night per person; the average price for a single room was $54. The big downtown hotels tended to be more expensive, but these hotels/motels also offered a wide variety of "extras" — limousine service, hotel-based shops and restaurants, color TV, cable movie channels, room service, etc.

The smaller hotels and motels that were located a distance away from the downtown area tended to be less expensive as well as less extravagant in the "extras" they offered.

At first Jerry and Lynn considered charging a standard price of $40 per night per person for their rooms, but some rooms were furnished more elegantly than others. Some rooms had their own private baths, some had nicer views. It seemed reasonable to charge different prices for different rooms. Also, their rooms were generally used by more than one person. So they decided to adjust their pricing methods a bit to reflect this. Here are the prices they finally came up with:

Room Numbers	Accommodations	Rates
1, 3, 5, & 6	Large rooms with views of the city, king-size beds, private bath, sitting area	Single $90 Double $95
2 & 4	Twin Beds	Single $55 Double $60
7 & 9	Queen-size Beds Shared Bath	Single $45 Double $50
8 & 10	King-size Beds Shared Bath	Single $45 Double $50

Summary

Pricing is mostly a matter of finding the right balance between your costs and your competition's prices and still making a fair profit. There are many factors to take into account when you are setting prices. You will lose your customers if your prices are too high. On the other hand, if your prices are to low, your profit may be too low for you to stay in business long. Setting prices is a very delicate part of a successful innkeeping business.

KEEPING FINANCIAL RECORDS

Keeping financial records is a must for any business. You need a clear way to keep track of your income and expenses. Good record keeping will help you plan and manage your inn intelligently and spot problems quickly.

Collecting the Money

When a guest checks out of the inn, you should fill out a receipt for the money paid and give the guest a copy. Guest receipts should be *itemized*. That means that you should write down the reasons for every charge such as parking, telephone calls, laundry, etc. A part of a sample guest receipt follows:

GUEST RECEIPT			
Guest's Name:			
Arrive:	Depart:	No. of Days:	Rate:
Item:	Charge:	Tax:	Total:
Grand Total:			

Some inns ask guests to put a deposit on their room in advance. This amount is then subtracted from the total bill when the guest checks out. Other inns may wait until the guest is ready to check out before they ask for payment. You may consider setting up a credit account for your *very regular guests*. Giving credit means that your guests don't have to pay at the end of each stay. Instead, you agree to keep a record and send them a bill later.

To Give or Not to Give Credit -- Credit Cards

If you're just starting out in your innkeeping business, you should make some arrangements with the major credit card companies such as American Express, visa, or MasterCard. This way, your guests can pay for their rooms with their credit cards, and you won't be responsible for handling a lot of cash or sending out bills. Credit card companies screen applicants, provide cards, and take responsibility for billing the customer. The major credit card companies "guarantee" payment of bills. This means the credit card company will pay the bill in full whether or not the customer has paid the company. The advantages of this credit system are that: 1) it is a convenient service for the customer; 2) it reduces *your* risk of giving credit; and 3) your money is not tied up in debts and unpaid bills.

Many inns, hotels/motels, and bed & breakfasts will use credit cards to "guarantee" reservations. This way when guests with reservations fail to show up, you won't be stuck with empty rooms and no profit. To participate in a major credit card plan, you usually have to pay the credit card company a certain percentage (usually 3%-4%) of all charged sales. In return, however, you get many benefits.

Easy Come, Easy Go -- The Daily Cash Sheet

Hopefully you will be receiving money every day that you are open. Many people will pay with a personal check or traveler's checks when they leave the inn. Credit card companies and individuals will be sending your checks in the mail to cover bills received during the past month. Keeping a daily record means that you'll know exactly what is going on in your business.

You will also have to pay your bills. While you may not do this every day, you will be doing it throughout the month. Your telephone bill may be due on one day, your gas and electric bill on another, and your laundry bill on yet another.

A daily cash sheet like this can be used to keep track of the money coming into and going out of your business every day. This form has been filled out for you so you can see how Jerry and Lynn keep track of their cash flow at the Bed & Breakfast Inn.

Daily Cash Sheet			
Cash Receipts		**Cash Payments**	
Cash Sales	$ 125.00	Salaries	$ 400.00
Credit Sales	$ 185.00	Building Expenses	-----
		Equipment & Furniture	$ 163.00
		Supplies	$ 57.00
		Advertising	-----
		Telephone	$ 179.43
		Garbage	42.75
		Other	-----
TOTAL:		**TOTAL:**	
CASH RECEIPTS:	**$310.00**	**CASH PAYMENTS:**	**$842.18**

As you can see, on this particular day Jerry and Lynn paid out more than they took in. But remember, the phone and garbage collection bills come only once a month. What matters is the cash left over at the end of the month.

To fill out this form, you add up all the money you received in a day -- the currency and checks from current guests and the checks received from past credit sales and enter these figures on the form.   Then look at the bills your unpaid out that day to the utility company, business supplies, laundry, etc., and add these up.

Daily cash sheets can be added up monthly and yearly. These figures are used to help fill out the profit/loss statement and the balance sheet. We will describe profit/loss statements in the next unit. If you do go into business for yourself, get the advice of an accountant about how to complete a balance sheet.

You probably know that there is much more to keeping records than this. You also have to complete employee records, payrolls, income forms, and others. Keeping records, rather than making your life harder, is supposed to make it easier.

Summary

Keeping good financial records is an important part of owning and operating the inn. Your bookkeeping system will be based on your guest receipts and bills. Keeping daily records of your income and expenses will show where you are spending money and how much you are taking and will help you plan for the success of your inn.

SUMMARY

This book has described the responsibilities of owning an inn. To start an inn, you need to do a significant amount of planning. First you have to be sure that owning a small business is right for you. Then you have to decide what services to offer, how to compete, and what legal requirements to meet.

To pick a good location, you have to find out if customers would use your inn. Then you have to get money to start. That means showing a banker that your idea is a good one.

Being in charge means dividing the work and hiring good workers. Then you must keep track of jobs to be done and who will do them.

Setting prices means figuring out the lowest price you can charge and also the highest price. To do this you need information on your expenses and on your competition's prices.

Advertising and selling are the ways you get customers. The good things your business does in town are called goodwill. These are all important ways to help your business succeed.

You should keep good financial records so you will know how the business is doing. Then you can decide if you can expand your business or if you need to cut it back.

In order to won and operate a successful inn, you need training, work experience, and the special business management skills we have covered in this module. If you have not had a course in hotel administration, you should take one before deciding to own an inn. You can learn business management skills through business classes, experience, or by using the advice and example of an expert.

You may not make a lot of money by owning an inn, however, you will have the personal satisfaction of being responsible for your business and making your own decisions. Think about how important these things are to you in considering whether you should start your own inn, hotel/motel, or bed & breakfast.

Appendix D

INSURANCE CHECKLIST

TYPE OF INSURANCE	PURCHASE	DO NOT PURCHASE
PROPERTY INSURANCE:		
Fire	_____	_____
Windstorm	_____	_____
Hail	_____	_____
Smoke	_____	_____
Explosion	_____	_____
Vandalism	_____	_____
Water Damage	_____	_____
Glass	_____	_____
LIABILITY INSURANCE	_____	_____
WORKERS' COMPENSATION	_____	_____
BUSINESS INTERRUPTION	_____	_____
DISHONESTY:		
Fidelity	_____	_____
Robbery	_____	_____
Burglary	_____	_____
Comprehensive	_____	_____
PERSONAL:		
Health	_____	_____
Life	_____	_____
Key Personnel	_____	_____

Special Marketing for a Bed & Breakfast Lodging Business

An Instructional Guide for Creating A Small Business
by Jerre G. Lewis, M.A.
& Leslie D. Renn, M.S.

Special Marketing for a
Bed & Breakfast Lodging Business

There are two ways of looking at a Bed & Breakfast lodging business—as a service organization, and as a marketing organization. A leading management authority stated, "If we want to know what a business is, we have to start with its purpose. And, its purpose must lie outside the business itself. In fact, it must lie in society, since a business enterprise is an organ of society. There is only one valid definition of a business purpose: to create a customer. Business actually has only two basic functions: marketing and innovation."

As manager of a Bed & Breakfast lodging business, you can create a customer through advertisement, sales promotion, and public relations. Behind each of these are: origination, imagination, appearance and appeal, salesmanship and hospitality.

Your guests determine what your business becomes. They convert economic resources into wealth when they rent rooms and buy meals and other goods and services. What your guests consider "value" and think they are buying determines what your business actually is, what it provides, and whether it will prosper.

Some important questions must be answered before marketing policy and investment decisions can be made:

- Who are the present guests? What do you know about them?

- Who are your potential customers and guests? Where do they live? What are their vacation and travel accommodation preferences?

- What are customer purchase habits and preferences for shopping, entertaining, etc., while at your resort, motel or hotel? What important accommodation needs do you not supply at the present time?

- What is your situation with competitors? What is your share of the present market?

- What are present and likely future trends in accommodations?

- What are the prospects for increasing business in the future?

- What kind(s) of marketing program(s) are needed? How implemented, etc.?

Careful review of these kinds of questions will give you the data needed to improve your marketing program.

Knowing Your Guest

To improve your marketing effectiveness, guest preferences must be known.

A guest questionnaire is the most useful and practical way to discover guest preferences. A simple, one-page form such as shown in Fig. 1 can be placed in each guest's room. Careful tabulation of the results over at least one season will yield useful information.

The room questionnaire can be supplemented with a personal, oral survey. A specific group of questions like, "How did you happen to stop here?" are asked of each guest. These are tabulated as soon as possible after the interview so that information is not lost. A good system is to list key questions at the left with a place for tabulation and typical remarks at the right.

A constant effort to survey guest preferences will pay off in increased guest satisfaction and success for your lodging business.

Guest Questionnaire

Dear Guest

Your assistance in helping us provide the very best in lodging and related services will be most valuable to us, and at the same time, help improve accommodations and services for yourself and other guests. Thank you.

1. Do you find this room attractive?   ☐ Yes   ☐ No

2. In what ways could we improve its appearance and appeal?

    _____

    _____

3. Is your room comfortable?   ☐ Yes   ☐ No

4. How could the room be made more comfortable?

    _____

    _____

5. Do you have any comments regarding the bath?

    _____

    _____

6. What about the room's equipment such as beds, lamps, radio, T.V. hangers, lights, etc.?

    _____

    _____

7. Do you have any other comments or suggestions?

    _____

    _____

Please place questionnaire in the attached envelope and leave on Desk. Thank you.

Manager

Every Employee — A Salesman

Among the essential concepts every employee should understand is that of "marketing." He must realize that the way he performs his job vitally affects the sales success of the business. He should understand the importance of improving the image of the business and the relationship of raises and promotions to business sales. The same concept should be inculcated into the mind of each department head. He should be convinced of his direct and indirect marketing responsibilities. The department head should then see that each employee under his supervision follows through as a marketer of the business.

Set Objectives—Plan the Program

A managerial study of marketing opportunities should lead to a list of objectives which appear to be attainable and specific marketing plans needed to meet them.

There are two types of marketing planning: 1) "end results", such as setting the advertising budget, and 2) "means to an end", or determining the courses of action which are to be taken to meet marketing goals or objectives.

Obviously, a close and interdependent relationship exists between these two types of planning. "End results" planning will affect the outcome of "means-to-an-end" planning.

A good marketing plan demands a clear definition of the various objectives and careful consideration of methods, policies, procedures and time.

Objectives should be separated as clearly and specifically as possible. Then, organize the methods, policies, and procedures which will apply to each objective. This will make it easier to tackle planning jobs directly with a minimum of confusion. For example, suppose you decide to improve direct mail advertising. One key "end result" plan might be to increase spring and fall occupancies 10 percent. Your "means-to-an-end" plan might suggest a quarterly newsletter. Specific planning could include 1) gathering samples of newsletters used by similar businesses, 2) planning the format of the newsletter, 3) deciding on the types of material to be used, 4) organizing the writing tasks, 5) obtaining a mailing list and 6) finding a creative printer who could do an excellent job at a reasonable price.

Determine Priorities

Establishing priorities for marketing planning is another important step. More easily attained objectives should be tackled first. There may be short range and long range plans and day-to-day plans. The success of short range and more easily attained plans will increase your confidence and ability to achieve more difficult and longer range plans.

Integrate Plans

Since each plan involves policies, budgets, procedures and programs, and each of these affect each other, all marketing plans should be integrated. This interdependence can make planning complex. Isolated plans are extremely restricted. If your marketing plans are well integrated, they will support each other and contain a consistency of purpose. The newsletter previously mentioned could support an expanded highway sign program and radio advertisement in cities where recipients of the newsletter reside.

Implement the Marketing Plan

Implementation of the marketing program will be influenced by the location, size, facilities, etc., of each individual business. It will also depend upon 1) relative importance of the various sales efforts to the business, 2) overall form of marketing organization which has been established for the business and 3) the number, placement, and diversity of marketing and sales activities carried on at various levels of the firm. There may be other "built-in" determinants of marketing methods, such as the philosophy of management and the type of clientele catered to.

Special Appendix

Web Site Marketing

Business Web Site
an
Effective Marketing Tool

More than 100 million people use the Internet each day. A website offers help in marketing your small business. Your web site can help level the playing field for small businesses who compete with big businesses. It can enable small business to expand their business nationally or internationally.

What makes a good web site?

A good web site shows by doing; it proves rather than states. Instead of making claims, it provides evidence.

Evidence can take several forms:

- Case Studies showing how your efforts solved a previous client's problems.

- Testimonials from satisfied clients.

- Reprints of articles you've written or reviews of your work.

Education, however, remains the best way to establish credibility. To the extent prospects leave your web site better informed about your product or service, the easier it is to gain their respect (and their purchase order).

Three steps to creating your own business web site.

Today's tools make web publishing accessible to small businesses without programming experience. For example, Microsoft® Publisher 97 includes PageWizard design assistants, web deign elements and design checkers to help your build a workable web site.

Step one:

Choose a structure and a look. Your site should be structured and designed to best tell your story. But where do you start? Using the Page Wizard, you can choose from pre-designed options that can later be customized so that establishing a structure and "look" is easy.

Step two:

Tell your story. Next, simply select the sample headlines and text provided and replace them with words that describe what you have to offer.

Step three:

Check your work and post your site. The design in Publisher 97 goes through your web site element by element, identifying potential problems. Then, the web publishing wizard guides you through the process of posting your web site on the local Internet service provider or on-line service of your choice.

Remember, with millions of web sites, you may have to market your web site as well as your small business to get traffic for your business. The web site can be an inexpensive way of effectively building your small business.

10 tips for Web Site Online Marketing

1. Put up a simple web page.
2. Use a name that will attract people
3. Give away advice and information
4. Have lots of e-mail correspondence
5. Provide customized pages for users.
6. Visit user groups
7. Get on mailing lists
8. Arrange links with related sites
9. Make sure you're in every possible directory
10. Do not "SPAM"

INDEX

Step-by-Step Guides To Start, Manage & Market Your Own Business

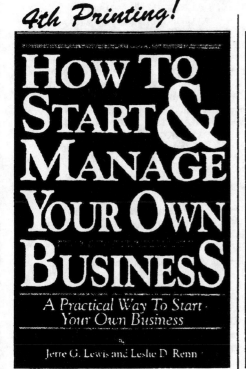
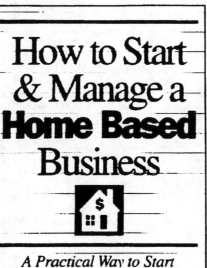
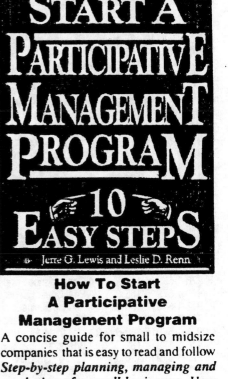

Business Books

Telephone 1-231-275-7287 • Fax 1-231-275-7242 • lewisjv@centurytel.net
Telephone 1-480-807-9530 • Fax 1-480-830-1187 • lrenn@cox.net

How to Start and Manage:

ISBN 978-1-57916-152-1	An Apparel Store Business
ISBN 978-1-57916-153-8	A Word Processing Service Business
ISBN 978-1-57916-154-5	A Garden Center Business
ISBN 978-1-57916-155-2	A Hair Styling Shop Business
ISBN 978-1-57916-156-9	A Bicycle Shop Business
ISBN 978-1-57916-157-6	A Travel Agency Business
ISBN 978-1-57916-158-3	An Answering Service Business
ISBN 978-1-57916-159-0	A Health Spa Business
ISBN 978-1-57916-160-6	A Restaurant Business
ISBN 978-1-57916-161-3	A Specialty Food Store Business
ISBN 978-1-57916-162-0	A Welding Business
ISBN 978-1-57916-163-7	A Day Care Center Business
ISBN 978-1-57916-164-4	A Flower and Plant Store Business
ISBN 978-1-57916-165-1	A Construction Electrician Business
ISBN 978-1-57916-166-8	A Housecleaning Service Business
ISBN 978-1-57916-167-5	A Nursing Service Business
ISBN 978-1-57916-168-2	A Bookkeeping Service Business
ISBN 978-1-57916-169-9	A Bed and Breakfast Business
ISBN 978-1-57916-170-5	A Secretarial Service Business
ISBN 978-1-57916-171-2	An Energy Specialist Business
ISBN 978-1-57916-172-9	A Guard Service Business
ISBN 978-1-57916-173-6	A Software Design Business
ISBN 978-1-57916-174-3	An Air Conditioning & Heating Business
ISBN 978-1-57916-175-0	A Plumbing Service Business
ISBN 978-1-57916-176-7	A Sewing Service Business
ISBN 978-1-57916-177-4	A Carpentry Service Business
ISBN 978-1-57916-178-1	A Home Attendent Service Business
ISBN 978-1-57916-179-8	A Tree Service Business
ISBN 978-1-57916-180-4	A Dairy Farming Business
ISBN 978-1-57916-181-1	A Farm Equipment Repair Service Business
ISBN 978-1-57916-182-8	A Children's Clothing Store Business
ISBN 978-1-57916-183-5	A Women's Apparel Store
ISBN 978-1-57916-184-2	A Convenience Food Store Business
ISBN 978-1-57916-185-9	A Pest Control Service Business
ISBN 978-1-57916-186-6	A Printing Business
ISBN 978-1-57916-187-3	An Ice Cream Business
ISBN 978-1-57916-188-0	A Mail Order Business
ISBN 978-1-57916-189-7	A Bookstore Business
ISBN 978-1-57916-190-3	A Home Furnishing Business
ISBN 978-1-57916-191-0	A Retail Florist Business
ISBN 978-1-57916-192-7	A Radio-Television Repair Shop Business
ISBN 978-1-57916-193-4	A Dry Cleaning Business
ISBN 978-1-57916-194-1	A Hardware Store Business
ISBN 978-1-57916-195-8	A Marine Retailing Business
ISBN 978-1-57916-196-5	An Office Products Business
ISBN 978-1-57916-197-2	A Pharmacy Business
ISBN 978-1-57916-198-9	A Fish Farming Business
ISBN 978-1-57916-199-6	A Personal Referral Service Business
ISBN 978-1-57916-200-9	A Solar Energy Business
ISBN 978-1-57916-201-6	A Building Service Contracting Business
ISBN 978-1-57916-202-3	A Retail Decorating Products Business
ISBN 978-1-57916-203-0	A Sporting Goods Store Business
ISBN 978-1-57916-204-7	A Retail Grocery Store
ISBN 978-1-57916-205-4	A Cosmetology Business
ISBN 978-1-57916-206-1	A Franchised Business
ISBN 978-1-57916-207-8	An Electronics Industry Consulting Practice Business
ISBN 978-1-57916-208-5	An Independent Consulting Practice Business
ISBN 978-1-57916-209-2	An Independent Trucking Business
ISBN 978-1-57916-210-8	An Accounting Service Business
ISBN 978-1-57916-211-5	A Nursery Business
ISBN 978-1-57916-212-2	A Seminar Promotion Business

ISBN 978-1-57916-231-9	A Bar & Cocktail Lounge Business
ISBN 978-1-57916-214-6	A Wheelchair Transportation Business
ISBN 978-1-57916-215-3	A Fertilizer and Pesticide Business
ISBN 978-1-57916-216-0	A Desktop Publishing Business
ISBN 978-1-57916-217-7	A Crime Prevention Business
ISBN 978-1-57916-218-4	A Gift Shop Business
ISBN 978-1-57916-219-1	A Handcraft Success Business
ISBN 978-1-57916-220-7	A Coin-Operated Laundries Business
ISBN 978-1-57916-221-4	A Property Management Business
ISBN 978-1-57916-222-1	An Auto Supply Store Business
ISBN 978-1-57916-223-8	A Men's Apparel Store Business
ISBN 978-1-57916-224-5	A Temporary Help Service Business
ISBN 978-1-57916-225-2	An Advertising Agency Business
ISBN 978-1-57916-226-9	A Firewood Sales Business
ISBN 978-1-57916-227-6	A Children's Bookstore Business
ISBN 978-1-57916-228-3	A Used Bookstore Business
ISBN 978-1-57916-229-0	A Sandwich Shop Deli Business
ISBN 978-1-57916-230-6	An Instant Print/Copy Shop
ISBN 978-1-57916-231-3	A Gift Specialty Store Business
ISBN 978-1-57916-232-0	A Gift Basket Service Business
ISBN 978-1-57916-233-7	A Hospitality Management Business
ISBN 978-1-57916-234-4	A Hotel Business
ISBN 978-1-57916-235-1	A Catering Service Business
ISBN 978-1-57916-236-8	A Carpet-Cleaning Service Business
ISBN 978-1-57916-237-5	A Window-Washing Service Business
ISBN 978-1-57916-238-2	An Innkeeping Service Business
ISBN 978-1-57916-239-9	An Apartment Preparation Service
ISBN 978-1-57916-240-5	A Kiosks and Cart Business
ISBN 978-1-57916-241-2	A Janitorial Service Business
ISBN 978-1-57916-242-9	A Medical Claims Processing Business
ISBN 978-1-57916-243-6	A Nursing Home Care Business
ISBN 978-1-57916-244-3	A Home Health Care Business
ISBN 978-1-57916-245-0	A Referral Services Business
ISBN 978-1-57916-246-7	A Hair Styling Salon Business
ISBN 978-1-57916-247-4	A Child Care Service Business

How-To Business Books

ISBN 978-1-57916-248-1	How to Buy and Sell A Business
ISBN 978-1-57916-249-8	How to Advertise A Small Business
ISBN 978-1-57916-250-4	How to Write A Successful Business Plan
ISBN 978-1-57916-251-1	How to Finance Your Business for the 21st Century
ISBN 978-1-57916-252-8	How to Market Your Business for the 21st Century
ISBN 978-1-57916-152-1	How to Start & Manage Your Own Business
ISBN 978-1-57916-152-1	How to Start & Manage a Home Based Business
ISBN 978-1-57916-152-1	How to Start a Participative Management Program

Library Discount - 20%
Retail Discount - 20%
$3.00 Postage & Handling
$21.95 Each
www.smallbusbooks.com

To Order Business Plans

Please Remit To:

Lewis & Renn Associates
10315 Harmony Drive
Interlochen, Michigan 49643

ISBN # _____ Title _____

ISBN # _____ Title _____

Name _____ Business Book _____

Address_____

City _____ U.S. Shipping & Postage **$ 3.00**

State_____ Zip _____

Total _____